Figure 1 - JERRI TUCK

EVERYTHING BY PRAYER

...in everything by prayer and supplication, with thanksgiving, let your requests be made known unto God – Phil. 4:6

By

Jerri Tuck

TRIBNET PUBLICATIONS

SACRAMENTO, CALIFORNIA

Everything By Prayer

TRIBNET PUBLICATIONS @

https://www.facebook.com/TribnetPublications/

SACRAMENTO, CALIFORNIA

PRINTED IN THE UNITED STATES OF AMERICA

© COPYRIGHT JERRI TUCK, 2019

ISBN-9781651499191

ALL IMAGES FROM WIKIPEDIA COMMONS, PUBLIC DOMAIN - UNLESS OTHERWISE NOTED

ALL SCRIPTURE TAKEN FROM THE NEW KING JAMES VERSION OF THE BIBLE UNLESS OTHERWISE NOTED

Table of Contents

Table of Figures vi
Dedication ix
Acknowledgements xv
PREFACE xvii
FOREWORD xix
Chapter 1 - RESTING IN THE ARK OF SAFETY 3
Chapter 2 - DELAYS ARE PART OF GOD'S TIMING 7
Chapter 3 - A DOG, A STAR, A PROMISE 13
Chapter 4 - BABY STEPS 21
Chapter 5 - WE LIVE IN A ZOO 27
Chapter 6 - I AM THE LORD THAT HEALS YOU 31
Chapter 7 - A TISKET, A TASKET 37
Chapter 8 - THE BLESSING OF GOD'S WORD 41
Chapter 9 - WHEN PRAYERS CONNECT 49
Chapter 10 - GOD CAN CHANGE THE GOVERNMENT ... 55
Chapter 11 - FROM MESS TO MESSAGE 61
Chapter 12 - LEARNING TO USE WISDOM 67
Chapter 13 - GROWING IN SPECIFIC FAITH 71
Chapter 14 - THE RAINS WILL COME TOMORROW 77
Chapter 15 - GOD AND THE WEATHER 83
Chapter 16 - WHETHER A MOLE HILL OR A MOUNTAIN ... 89
Chapter 17 - WELCOME TO WVMG 95
Chapter 18 - SO, YOU WANT TO SPEAK HEBREW? OY VEY! ... 101
Chapter 19 - IT PAYS TO ADVERTISE 109
Chapter 20 - IS THERE A CHRISTIAN FLAG? 115
Chapter 21 - DEFINITELY NOT MISTAKEN IDENTITY ... 123

Chapter 22 - HOW DO YOU EAT AN ELEPHANT?................................. 131
Chapter 23 - THREE RESURRECTIONS... 139
Chapter 24 - MAKING LIFE COUNT FOR ETERNITY............................ 147
About the Author & Jerri's Books... 151

Table of Figures

Figure 1 - JERRI TUCK i
Figure 2 - "PATCHWORK FAMILY" By Jerri Tuck viii
Figure 3 – Tamala – Debi's Child ix
Figure 4 - Shelly, Shannon, Jeremy & Sheri Lynn – David's Children x
Figure 5 - Kacie and Brandon - John's Children x
Figure 6 - Britton and Bailey - Jeff's Children xi
Figure 7 - Amber and Mallory - Sandy's Children xi
Figure 8 – (L-R) Zach, Isaac, Eli, Graycen, & Levi - Virginia's Children xii
Figure 9 - Carson, Sheridan, & Charla - Dotty's Children xii
Figure 10 – Brody, Jaxon, & Ayden - Alan's Children xii
Figure 11 - "EVERYTHING BY PRAYER" xiii
Figure 12 - Jerri with Doug (L) and Charlie (R) xv
Figure 13 - Sandy Sage - Jerri's Daughter xvii
Figure 14 - JERRI AT HER BOOK TABLE 2
Figure 15 - MOUNT ARARAT - NOAH'S ARK LANDED THERE 3
Figure 16 - 2005 CHINA MISSION TEAM – 7
Figure 17 - ROOFTOP MINISTRIES CHINA 11
Figure 18 - TUCK REALTY CORP. 13
Figure 19 - HAVE YOU SEEN A LITTLE BLACK AND WHITE DOG? 16
Figure 20 - JERRI BY JORDAN RIVER WITH ELAN AND LIOR - 1994 18
Figure 21 - FOUR SEASONS 21
Figure 22 - WE LIVE IN A ZOO 27
Figure 23 - GOD DOES THE HEALING, BUT... 31
Figure 24 - EASTER BASKETS 37
Figure 25 - COURTHOUSE & THE BIBLE READING MARATHON 41
Figure 26 - 4-27-07 - PRESCHOOL CHOIR AT BRM 44
Figure 27 - PASTOR HUTCHINGS - EMCEE - 2004 BRM 46
Figure 28 - GEORGIA STATE SENATOR ROSS TOLLISON AT BRM 47
Figure 29 - HOME BIBLE STUDY MIDDLE GEORGIA COLLEGE 49
Figure 30 - CIVIL WAR CEMETRY - MACON-COCHRAN HWY 52
Figure 31 - DOTTY & VIRGINIA IN THEIR YOUNGER DAYS 55
Figure 32 - DOTTY AND VIRGINIA GROWN UP 58
Figure 33 - THE TUCK'S NEW HOME 61
Figure 34 - WILSON & CORA - PHILIPPINE MISSIONARIES AT OLD HOUSE 65
Figure 35 - JERRI'S SCOFIELD REFERENCE BIBLE 67
Figure 36 - INDIAN ORPHAN WITH JERRI - 1997 71
Figure 37 - KUALA LUMPUR - MALASIA 75
Figure 38 - JERRI PREACHING AT CRUSADE IN INDIA 77
Figure 39 - TEE SHIRTS & SUNGLASSES FOR INDIAN ORPHANS - 1997 ... 79
Figure 40 - TYPICAL MONSOON RAINS IN INDIA 81
Figure 41 - Ominous Clouds Over Bleckley County Courthouse 83
Figure 42 – TORNADO COMING OUR WAY 84

Figures

Figure 43 – PINE TREE DANGEROUSLY CLOSE TO THE HOUSE 86
Figure 44 - WHETHER A MOLE HILL OR A MOUNTAIN 89
Figure 45 - WAS IT THE TINKER BELL FAIRY? 93
Figure 46 - IN THE WVMG STUDIO - (L-R) KRISTY CRANFORD, VIRGINIA TUCK, SARAH TYSON, DOTTY TUCK & HONG VO 95
Figure 47 - MY NAME IS ON THE ROLL 96
Figure 48 - MY FEET ARE ON THE ROCK - JESUS 98
Figure 49 - JERRI IN ISRAEL WITH IDF SOLDIERS 101
Figure 50 - JERRI WITH SISTER KATHY 104
Figure 51 PATCHWORK FAMILY - 25 COPIES PLEASE 106
Figure 52 - "JESUS IS LORD" SIGN NORTH OF COCHRAN, GA 109
Figure 53 - "JESUS IS LORD" SIGN SOUTH OF COCHRAN (L-R) JUNE SMITH, CAROLYN WILLIAMS, & EMILY DENNIS 112
Figure 54 - CHRISTIAN FLAG ON BLECKLEY COUNTY COURTHOUSE ... 115
Figure 55 - CITY HALL FLAG RAISING - 2012 117
Figure 56 - CHRISTIAN FLAG OVER COCHRAN CITY HALL 119
Figure 57 - LAURA WILLIAMS BRM COORDINATOR, NIGERIA 123
Figure 58 - FEAR IS A LIAR ROCK 125
Figure 59 - POSTER FOR BRM NIGERIA 126
Figure 60 - PRESENTED BRM CERTIFICATE FOR READING THE BIBLE TO JOSHUA MEETING 128
Figure 61 - THEY TRAVELED THREE HOURS TO READ THE BIBLE 130
Figure 62 - 2 CHRONICLES 7:14 131
Figure 63 - DIANNE BENTLEY FROM IOWA 133
Figure 64 - GOD'S WORD OVER THE WORLD - JULY 14 134
Figure 65 - JERRI WITH COUNTY MAP OF GEORGIA 136
Figure 66 - BLECKLEY PROBATION DETENTION CENTER - COCHRAN... 139
Figure 67 - COBY AND DOROTHY DANIEL 142
Figure 68 - LAZARUS, COME FORTH! 144
Figure 69 - GONE FISHIN' By Jerri Tuck 151
Figure 70 - PATCHWORK FAMILY - By Jerri Tuck 152
Figure 71 - "JUST JERRI" - By Jerri Tuck 153
Figure 72 - LETTER FOR THE COG HALL OF CHRISTIAN EXCELLENCE 2004 154
Figure 73 - CHARLIE & JERRI TUCK - NEARLY 50 YEARS SERVING THE LORD 155

Figure 2 - "PATCHWORK FAMILY" By Jerri Tuck

Dedication

This book is lovingly dedicated to the Tuck grandchildren!

When Charlie and I combined our families on September 29, 1972 we had no idea that one day we would be able to count 22 grandchildren in our Tuck Tribe. These precious children, many of whom are now adults with children of their own, are truly arrows into the future.

To begin with we said, "Eight is enough!" At the time, Charlie had five children and I had three children. Then along came Alan Raffield, who joined the tribe, and the count went up to nine!

With this many children you can just imagine there would be some dysfunction and you would be correct. There were some divorces and remarriages, which caused our grandchildren count to go up a little bit, but all in all we are blessed with every one of these kids, whom we consider part of the Tuck Tribe. Only one of our children (Linda) was never blessed with children, but she has sure had some cute little canine pets!

Figure 3 – Tamala – Debi's Child

Figure 4 - Shelly, Shannon, Jeremy & Sheri Lynn – David's Children

Figure 5 - Kacie and Brandon - John's Children

Dedication

Figure 6 - Britton and Bailey - Jeff's Children

Figure 7 - Amber and Mallory - Sandy's Children

Figure 8 – (L-R) Zach, Isaac, Eli, Graycen, & Levi - Virginia's Children

Figure 9 - Carson, Sheridan, & Charla - Dotty's Children

Figure 10 – Brody, Jaxon, & Ayden - Alan's Children

Dedication

My prayer is that all our grandchildren will realize the amazing power of prayer in their lives and in the lives of their children. We serve a living and real God. His eyes are not shut, and His ears are not closed to the cries of His children.

With love and devotion,

Grandma Jerri Tuck

Figure 11 - "EVERYTHING BY PRAYER"

Confess your faults one to another, and pray one for another, that ye may be healed. The effectual fervent prayer of a righteous man availeth much.
James 5:16

Acknowledgements

There's not enough paper or ink to acknowledge all those who have contributed in being an answer to our prayers; but over and above all the special people who are in our beloved family and those we count as friends, is the extraordinary God we serve. Without Him the events of this book could have never happened.

Charlie Tuck, the man whom I have shared life with for over 47 years, is not only my very best friend and confidant, he is also my main editor in reading over the books I've written and also the weekly column I write for several local newspapers. His dedication to make me look good on the printed page can never be underestimated.

I would also like to thank my precious brother, Doug Krieger whose constant encouragement and expertise in literary endeavors has pushed me to complete another book. Doug is one of the finest Christians on the planet, with a consuming love for our Lord. He and I both gave our hearts to Jesus (along with our younger brother, Dwight) in 1957. It has been quite a journey and we know the 'best' is yet to come!

With Love in Christ,

Jerri Tuck

Figure 12 - Jerri with Doug (L) and Charlie (R)

Everything By Prayer

PREFACE

Sometimes when you've walked with the Lord for a long time, you begin to take for granted that God hears and answers your prayers. You just walk with Him and talk with Him and He becomes as real as the one seated next to you in church, or the one who walks beside you day by day.

One day I shared an answer to prayer with our daughter, Sandy Sage. After hearing the amazing thing God had done for us (in answer to prayer) she replied, "Mom you never told me that before."

Figure 13 - Sandy Sage - Jerri's Daughter

I began thinking, "I bet there are a lot of things I've never shared with her before!" The next morning, as I sat meditating in my study, within the space of ten minutes the Holy Spirit shared over twenty, very special, answers to prayer that I had received over the years. I was writing them down just as fast as He was giving them to me.

When I looked over the list of answers to prayer, I realized these needed to be shared, not only with Sandy, but with other people as well. Sometimes people think that God doesn't care about them. They feel their problems are so insignificant that God would never take the time to concern Himself with their problem. Not so! God cares about everything that concerns us.

Through this little book you will discover that whether it's a mountain you're facing or something as small as a molehill that is giving you trouble, God cares. If you're a non-believer and think all these 'so-called answers to prayer' are only coincidences, I pray you will be drawn to the Lord who created you and loved you so much that He sent His only Son to die for you.

Thanks, Sandy, for being a springboard for my latest book, EVERYTHING BY PRAYER!

Jerri Tuck

Cochran, Georgia

FOREWORD

By

Douglas W. Krieger

Each new publication Jerri Tuck releases through Tribnet Publications is always a blessing for me, her brother—both as my sister in real life and as a sister in Christ. You never know what will be produced by the pen of this ready writer.

I was especially delighted to work on her text, **Everything By Prayer**, because, on the one hand, it integrates some of her material from her previous books, but on the other hand, adds so much more to her journey and the answers to prayer over and over again in which her Lord and Savior manifests His presence on her behalf, her family's, the rest of the Household of Faith, and the world around Jerri.

You're not going to want to put this little book down—why? Because each page is jammed packed with true accounts of how God is so real if we simply move into EVERYTHING by prayer. Anxiety, worry, frustration, and grief are swallowed up as we engage in conversation with the God of the universe. Yes, our Father longs for His people to unceasingly petition the Father on behalf of His children.

There's a whole lot of thanksgiving mixed with prayer given to our Father Who knows exactly what is needed in whatever circumstance we find ourselves . . . thanking Him ahead of time for the answers displays a welcomed trust in Him Who longs for each one of us to rest in His faithfulness to answer in His perfect timing.

I believe this addition to Jerri's "works" will be of inestimable blessing to so many who have begun the journey with Christ but fail to keep the "inner eyes of their hearts" fixed on Him.

After Jesus' resurrection He did not directly address over a million people gathered in Jerusalem during Passover to declare "I'm alive!" No, He exchanged the events of the past week with two on the road to Emmaus and held a private Bible study with them expounding all the Scriptures from Moses and all the Prophets the things concerning Himself (Luke 24:27).

Yes, their hearts burned within them *"while He talked with us on the road, and while He opened the Scriptures to us"* (Luke 24:32)—and that's precisely what prayer is all about: Seeing and listening to Jesus reveal Himself in His Word; generating the kind of faith that will run back to Jerusalem to tell the disciples *"about the things that had happened on the road, and how He was recognized to them in the breaking of bread"* (Luke 24:35).

This is Jerri's road she's taken with Jesus—He's revealed to her those things concerning Himself from His Word . . . things that happened on the road. I believe you too will recognize this Jesus who longs to fellowship with us in our triumphs and despairs.

Welcome to Jerri's world—you won't be disappointed because Jesus will show up and expound all the Scriptures about Himself until your heart will burn within you in the breaking of the bread! He longs to hear and to answer—yes, and He longs to hear you and answer your petitions with thanksgiving! If this book doesn't enflame your heart in prayer—then it will have failed its charge: Turn you to Jesus where **everything by prayer** is your experience each day.

I know you will enjoy this blessed accounting of real answers to prayer from Jerri's pen—may they stir within your spirit an uninterrupted exchange with God Who really does desire we bring to Him all things—everything by prayer and supplication.

Douglas W. Krieger, Jerri's brother

Sacramento, California

Christmas/Hanukkah, 2019

EVERYTHING BY PRAYER!

By

Jerri Tuck

Figure 14 - JERRI AT HER BOOK TABLE

Chapter 1 - RESTING IN THE ARK OF SAFETY

*"And the ark rested in the seventh month,
on the seventeenth day of the month,
upon the mountains of Ararat."*
Genesis 8:4

Figure 15 - MOUNT ARARAT - NOAH'S ARK LANDED THERE

This was the third time in our sixteen-year marriage that my husband had left me, and it was to be the final time! Things couldn't look any darker for a young woman in her early thirties with three little children, ages 10, 8 and 1.

The note read simply, "I'm gone and it's all your fault!" After the initial shock wore off, I took stock of my situation and it wasn't very promising. For starters I had no money, no job, no car, very little food and no way to make a house payment.

After throwing myself on the floor in a fit of helpless tears the Lord told me to get up and get in His Word. Opening my Bible to a Scripture in Isaiah, I read, *"Can a woman forget her sucking child, that she should not have compassion on the son of her womb? Yea, they may forget, yet will I not forget thee. Behold I have engraved thee upon the palms of my hands; thy walls are continually before me"* (Isaiah 49:15-16).

Without question I knew the Lord would be taking care of me, because I knew that when He looked at those nail prints, my name was engraved there for all eternity. What an incredible promise!

It's very hard to explain how a person can be facing an impossible situation, but still be at peace. As day after day went by, I poured over the words in my Bible. I just knew there had to be an answer for this journey I was on. One day I stumbled across the words in Genesis 8 where it was recorded simply that, *"God remembered Noah!"*

I put myself in that ark with Noah that day. What was it like to be cooped up for a year or more? It must have been dark and surely there was the awful smell of the animals coming up from the lower decks to contaminate the air. Cramped? Absolutely. Frustrated? Most likely. That's where I found myself, but just knowing that God hadn't forgotten me caused me to realize that all I had to do was trust Him.

Interestingly we read that the waters kept rising, but no matter how high they rose, the ark rested on top of the waters. Somehow that hit home with me. Things didn't necessarily get easier, but I was no longer floundering... I was resting in the ark of safety.

As I prayed for provisions they came in such unexpected ways. I had led a young woman, who was studying to become a beauty operator, to the Lord. Naturally she needed someone to try out new hairstyles and I was her guinea pig. Twice a week I had a new hairdo!

Friends realized the seemingly dire situation I was in and one evening I was surprised by a group who brought food and furniture. Then to top it off one of the friends had an extra vehicle to loan me... a white Cadillac! I was styling.

As I drove the Cadillac to church each Sunday, I wondered how in the world I would be able to afford the gas. In 1972 gas was averaging about $ .33 a gallon. One day I pulled up to the gas station and asked the attendant to put $1 worth of gas in the tank. As he was pumping gas, I leaned over my steering wheel and prayed, "Lord, how am I ever going to do this? Lord, please help me."

The attendant came to my window and said, "I filled it up for you lady!" I was horrified. I only had $1 and I didn't know what to do except to shake my head, with tears streaming down my face.

Then he added, "Don't worry about it. The gas is on me!"

Well, that did it! God was showing me that He could take care of me. The ark of safety was Him; not a 485-foot vessel of wood, but a God who was bigger than the universe. I knew in my heart that He was the Creator of everything, and He was truly in charge of my life. He could and would provide.

Delving into the construction of the ark I found that it was not only large enough to house all the animals ordained for rescue; it was also three stories high. What a perfect picture of our God. Safety was real because of the three-in-one God.

As I traveled with my three little girls in those early days of loneliness and darkness, I felt safe. There would be a good ending for me. God was in control! The God who engraved me upon the palms of his hands, had secured me within the true 'ark of safety', and He would one day place me on solid ground and put a rainbow in my future.

Amazingly the Bible says that the ancient ark of Noah's day landed on the 17th day of the month on Mt. Ararat. The Lord Jesus Christ was crucified on the 14th day and resurrected on the 17th day of the month Nisan.

In his *Journey to Arzrum* Russian poet Aleksandr Pushkin recounted his travels to the Caucasus in 1828-1829 to visit Mt. Ararat and said, "I went out of the tent into the fresh morning air. The sun was rising. Against the clear sky one could see a white-snowcapped, twin-peaked mountain. 'What mountain is that?' I asked, stretching myself, and heard the answer: 'That's Ararat.' What a powerful effect a few syllables can have! Avidly I looked at the Biblical mountain, saw the ark moored to its peak with the hope of regeneration and life, saw both the raven and dove, flying forth, the symbols of punishment and reconciliation......" *

According to scientists Mt. Ararat has an ice cap on its summit and it has been melting since 1957. This was the year I was saved and truly the mountain of punishment and reconciliation is dissolving before my eyes. Death is over and resurrection life has begun and will one day be fully realized when I step over into glory.

* *Pushkin, Aleksandr (1974). A Journey to Arzrum. Translated by Birgitta Ingemanson. Ann Arbor: Ardis. p. 50. ISBN 978-0882330679.*

Chapter 2 - DELAYS ARE PART OF GOD'S TIMING

"My times are in Thy hand."
Psalm 31:15

Figure 16 - 2005 CHINA MISSION TEAM –
(L-R) Tiffany Crumpler, Beth Dunn, Virginia Alligood,
Jerri Tuck, Jane Tuten, Kelli McGinnis

The year was 1957 and I had jumped feet first into an organization called Child Evangelism Fellowship. Don and Jewel Morsey, the couple who brought me to Christ, were very involved in this outreach ministry to the children in their neighborhood.

Shortly after I was saved, I began to help Jewel in her weekly Good News Club. My very first job for God was to sit next to her preschool son Miles and keep him from throwing bread over the flannel board as his mom put the Bible figures on the board.

After several months I began to think that I could also be a teacher, so I invited 100 children in my mother's neighborhood to come to my first Good News Club. Two little girls, Barbara and Bonnie McCranie showed up. Both asked Jesus in their hearts and I was on my way. I felt I had 100% success that day and thus began my love for reaching children with the Gospel.

Soon it was time for the 1958 California State Fair. I was thrilled to be part of an outreach in the Child Evangelism booth. Dressed in a white blouse and a homemade skirt with panels the colors of the Wordless Book; I encouraged little children to come into our tent so I could tell them the glorious story of salvation.

Eagerly the children listened as I opened my little paper Wordless Book and told them the best part first. The end of the book had a *gold* page and I told them about the beauties in Heaven; complete with the passage about the street of the city being pure gold.

Little eyes grew wide as I told them the sad news of sin, represented by the *black* page. Yes, even little children are sinners and need a Savior. What great news unfolded as I turned the page to *red*, the color of the blood of the Lord Jesus and the *white* page, depicting His amazing resurrection after three days in a tomb.

As child after child left the tent, I rejoiced that many of them had made the decision to ask Jesus to be their personal Savior. The *green* cover of the little Wordless Book was to encourage them to *grow* in the Lord by reading the New Testaments that I gave to each of them. Each child also got a little Wordless Book so they could share the story with others.

The fair lasted several weeks and what fun I and the other CEF workers had sharing Jesus with hundreds and hundreds of boys and girls. Adults also came along and visited with us at our booth. Many of them sat at the back of the tent listening right along with the children. Only the Lord knows how many of them also gave their hearts to the Lord.

One afternoon a very small woman stopped by, showing great interest in what we were doing. As it turned out she was a child evangelist herself and was getting ready to make a trip to Kowloon, China.

How my heart thrilled as I heard her tell of her rooftop ministry. She told me of hundreds of children who crowded on the rooftops of the high-rise buildings, eager to hear the stories of the Bible.

Seeing I was enthralled with her stories she told me she would be leaving soon on a freighter for China. Then with a twinkle in her eye she said, "Would you like to come with me?"

"Would I?" I was already mentally packing my bag to make the trip halfway around the world. My plans and my husband's plans however didn't quite sync about me making a trip to China. I decided I better just put that idea on the shelf and instead started reading every book I could about missions to China.

Hudson Taylor, one of the first missionaries to China truly inspired me, especially when God spoke to him and said, "Hudson, I'm going to evangelize China. Do you want to come along?" I could just see this 19th Century man, pulling himself up to his full height, giving God a snappy salute and saying, "Yes, Sir! I am ready to go!"

Other stories enthralled me . . . the stories of John and Betty Stam, C.T. Studd, Jonathon Goforth and countless others challenged me about the millions of lost Chinese. Oh, why wouldn't my husband let me go? My prayers for China filled my waking thoughts. Lord, save China!

One day the phone rang and a voice, thick with an accent said, "Hello. This is Reverend Fung. Are you Jerri?"

Confused and yet at that same time excited, because I immediately surmised with a name like *Fung* this had to be someone of Asian descent, I answered, "Yes."

"I understand you are a child evangelist. Someone told me about you," he said. "I am the pastor of a Chinese church in downtown Sacramento and I need help with the 4th grade girl's class. Would you be interested in helping us?"

I can't begin to tell you how elated I was when my husband told me I could teach this class. I guess he figured I would be safer there in downtown Sacramento than on a freighter headed to China! Reverend Fung had a huge church with 900 children enrolled in classes.

Sunday after Sunday, teaching these little girls, was such a blessing. Even after the Lord moved me into another area of ministry, I realized that my burden for China was just God's way of getting me ready for Rev. Fung's church. After a year of teaching these children, the Lord moved me on to another area of service and the dream of China faded.

Other dreams also faded in the next few years; dreams of a happy home and a loving husband. It was not to be. Learning how to pick up the pieces of a broken marriage and shattered dreams were not easy, but I knew God was with me. Although the seas were stormy, I was not on a freighter, I was safe in the ARK! I had nothing to fear.

One day the Lord sent an amazing man into my life who became my true counterpart in every way. In 2005, when we had been married thirty-three years, Charlie's youngest daughter Virginia, now a beautiful young woman, who had a heart for China, invited me to go on a mission trip with her to smuggle bibles to the Chinese Underground Church.

Taking a deep breath, I asked my husband if I could go with her and what a delight when he told me I could go with his blessing.

What an adventure we had. We packed bibles in backpacks and somehow made it through airport security. Flying down to the island of Hainan we boarded a van and headed for town. Unexpectedly the van stopped. We managed to swallow our fears when we saw some men running toward us down a small mountainside. They opened the back doors of our van and took the backpacks. None of us moved or made a sound.

Delays are Part of God's Timing

Figure 17 - ROOFTOP MINISTRIES CHINA

Off we went to a hotel and the next night six members of the Underground Church came to express their appreciation for what we had done in bringing them 'bread'.

Later, after delivering more bibles, we drove up to the north of the island and flew back to Hong Kong. The following day we boarded a bus to do some sightseeing. What a shock I got when we crossed a bridge that had a sign that read, "KOWLOON".

God's delays do not necessarily mean he is telling us 'No." Sometimes He is telling us to wait. Timing is all up to Him. When we leave things in His hands, to work out in His time, we will experience Him in the most amazing way.

When I saw that sign, I realized that my times were most certainly in His capable hands. I could trust Him to work everything out. His timing is always perfect!

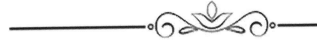

Chapter 3 - A DOG, A STAR, A PROMISE

"For there is nothing covered, that shall not be revealed; neither hid, that shall not be known."
Luke 12:2

Figure 18 - TUCK REALTY CORP.

My 28 years in real estate was quite an adventure. Early on the Lord told me that if I would let Him work through me, my office would become a soul saving station. That word from God confirmed to me that I was in the right line of work in the little town of Cochran, Georgia.

Real estate in a small town with only 12,000 people in the entire county has its distinct advantages. Nearly all my clients eventually became friends or fellow church members and 60-65% became repeat customers when it was time to sell or buy again.

One day a very dignified looking couple came into my office to discuss some properties I had listed on beautiful Lake

Everything by Prayer

Linda, an upscale area of Cochran. As they sat in front of my desk, they couldn't help but notice a fairly, large plaque on the wall behind me that loudly proclaimed in psychedelic colors, CLAP YOUR HANDS! JESUS IS LORD!

It was always interesting to see how 'religious' people would get when they read those words. This couple was no exception. The man began to tell me all about his experience as a church member and how much he enjoyed church functions. I smiled and hoped that I was going to make more friends and maybe even make a sale before the week was over. Before they left my office, an appointment was all set up for early the next morning to go house hunting.

At 7:30 a.m. sharp we met at a beautiful two-story home right on lake front property. I think this was the earliest I had ever shown a house; the dew was still thick on the freshly mowed lawn.

The gentleman was very conscientious about not tracking grass into the house; he respectfully removed his shoes before entering. For the next forty-five minutes we went from room to room as I pointed out all the wonderful features of the home, as well as the pluses of lakefront property.

Feeling quite confident that a sale might be forthcoming I was inwardly congratulating myself on doing a great job of showing the house, until we went outside. That's when my sale started going downhill in a big and unexpected way!

When the prim and proper gentleman walked outside, he looked both ways, bent over and picked up one shoe and said, "Where's my shoe?"

I was horrified. His other shoe was missing.

Then he got louder and said, "Son of a gun! Where's my shoe?? No! I mean, son-of-a-_ _ _ _ _!"

I was so flustered I didn't know what to say except to stutter out, "I . . . I'm so sorry."

"Those are my favorite shoes," he sputtered. Then, totally frustrated he went stomping all around the house in his white socks, now covered in grass, with one shoe in hand. When he came back to where his horrified wife and I were standing he said, "Let's go and look at the next house."

"Uh," I said, "would you like to go home first and get another pair of shoes?"

Obviously exasperated he said, "Okay. We'll meet you there in 30 minutes."

As I watched him drive off in frustration and anger, I had no clue how to fix this problem. It wasn't covered in Real Estate 101. All I could think to do was to pray a Scripture that I often claimed when I misplaced or lost something. "Lord, your Word says that there is nothing covered that shall not be revealed or hidden that shall not be made manifest. I pray right now that you will reveal to me where that man's shoe is. Lord, I believe YOU know where that shoe is and I'm counting on YOU to lead me to it!"

Just then, as I walked to my car, I saw the next-door neighbor come outside to pick up her morning paper. I went over to her and explained the awful situation about the missing shoe. She said, "Jerri, I think I saw a little black and white dog running down the street with a shoe in his mouth." She pointed left and I was on my way.

Rounding the curve in the road I came to a boat ramp. I saw an elderly gentleman and a young teenage boy getting ready to put their boat in the water. Jumping out of my car, knowing I only had 30 minutes before I had to meet the couple, I breathlessly asked, "Have either of you seen a little black dog with a shoe in his mouth?"

The old man shook his head 'no', but the young teenager grinned big and said, "Yes. I saw him." Pointing to another street he said, "He went that-a-way!"

Now I was on the hunt. "Thank you, Lord. I know your Word is true. I'm going to find that dog AND that shoe."

Figure 19 - HAVE YOU SEEN A LITTLE BLACK AND WHITE DOG?

As I drove up another street, I saw a garage door open and there, sitting as pretty, as you please, was a little black and white dog. When he saw me get out of my car he started barking. I stood with my hands on my hips and looked him square in the eye and said, "Alright you little mutt. Where is that shoe?" No answer, so of course I went to the door.

I knocked a few times, but no one came to the door. By this time the thieving little mutt had decided to run in search of another shoe. I glanced around the garage and there, right in front of me on top of a barbeque pit, was my client's shoe!

Believe me, I was praising God all the way to the next house where I jumped out of the car and with the shoe behind my back, I pertly asked the couple, "Do you believe in prayer?" Then I proceeded to tell them that when I misplaced or lost something, I always claimed a favorite Scripture. I then shared the Bible verse and proudly presented my client with his shoe!

The man was in shock. He examined the shoe from heel to toe and there wasn't a single tooth mark. Then he topped off the whole adventure by saying, "These are my favorite shoes and they're Hush Puppies!"

Later that day his wife called to talk with me, but I wasn't home. She then asked my husband about where the Bible verse was located that I had used to find her husband's shoe. Charlie said, "I'm not sure where it is in the Bible, but I do know she uses that verse all the time when she loses things."

Through the years I have lost items as common as a set of car keys and as valuable as my precious Star of David necklace. Each time the Lord has been faithful to help me in my search. Some answers come quickly, but as in the case of my favorite necklace it took seven years!

My precious stepmother, Margie Krieger, passed away in 1994. She was the first person who witnessed to me about the Lord Jesus Christ. Although I fought her tooth and toenail, I eventually gave in to her gentle and sometimes scary pleadings.

In 1957 she convinced me that Jesus was going to return to earth in judgment and because I was such a bad sinner I was going to be in big trouble. God sent me a dream that judgment had come. I was swimming in a sea of blood. The dream scared me so bad that I went to a home Bible study with her and on that very first night the Lord became my personal Savior.

Margie and I had a very special bond and when she passed away in 1994, she left me a monetary inheritance that was such a blessing to my husband and me. We were able to pay bills, invest and even share with others.

While on a mission trip to Israel that same year, I used a portion of my inheritance to purchase a beautiful Star of David in her memory. There were 30 small diamonds on the gold star. Oh, my how I loved that necklace.

Seven years passed and I wore it every day and night and only occasionally removed it at night. Many, many times while clasping the star, I would thank the Lord for Margie and for her persistence in continuing to witness to me.

Everything by Prayer

Figure 20 - JERRI BY JORDAN RIVER WITH ELAN AND LIOR - 1994

Then it happened. The necklace was gone. I was frantic. I looked everywhere and to no avail. I was sure the grandchildren had played with it and lost it. Maybe I vacuumed it and it was gone forever, but I just couldn't believe it. I prayed and claimed Luke 12:2. This went on for years. I just couldn't let it go.

Knowing how much I loved that necklace Charlie even bought me another one with little diamonds at the tip of each triangle . . . but it wasn't the same. It just wasn't the same.

Then one day, after seven years, I accidentally pulled the drawer of my jewelry box all the way out and you guessed it! There it was, safe and sound and waiting for me to discover it.

I ran with unspeakable joy out the back door to Charlie's workshop. "You'll never guess what I found," I said with tears streaming down my face.

He knew. He could tell by the joy on my face. "You found your Star of David!!" We hugged and hugged. God's Word is true. It's true in 1985 (the Hush Puppy shoe), in 2008 (the Star of David necklace) and in whatever year you're reading this book. You can count on it.

As a postscript to this story, a financial calamity almost happened. I misplaced a check for $2,000 which was made out to Charlie from our insurance company as a portion of the payment on his new hearing aids.

For two days we searched and searched. I even went out in the dead of night and emptied bags of garbage covered with ants, looking for the missing check. I kept telling the Lord that there was no way this could happen when I had just told the world that His Word (Luke 12:2) was my assurance that He would help me find lost items.

"Lord, I believe Your Word that there is nothing covered that shall not be revealed or hidden that shall not be made known! Lord, you wouldn't let me write a chapter like that and not keep Your Word!!"

Charlie was an absolute prince about my losing the check. "Honey, we'll just call the insurance company and if they won't send another check, we'll just pay it ourselves. It's okay."

What a guy!

I'm glad to report that the Lord honored His Word AGAIN! While putting away some napkins in a cupboard full of Tupperware, I saw a few pieces of paper. Although the papers were only stray recipes, I looked deeper into the cupboard and there was the insurance check . . . in perfect condition! Believe me I went straight to the bank and deposited that check.

I love it when I can brag on God!

Everything by Prayer

Chapter 4 - BABY STEPS

*"But grow in grace, and in the knowledge of our Lord and Savior, Jesus Christ.
To Him be glory both now and forever. Amen."*
2 Peter 3:18

Figure 21 - FOUR SEASONS

When Charlie and I married in 1972, there were some folks in our church that didn't give our marriage six months. After all, Charlie had just been delivered and saved from a life of alcoholism only five months before and between us we had eight children, seven of whom lived with us in a small, 1,200 SF house.

Even back in 1972 a paycheck of $242.00 every two weeks wasn't a lot to live on. The courts had ordered my ex-husband to pay $33.00 a month per child, which added up to a whopping $99.00 a month. We were living by faith, especially when my ex only made payments for a few months and then headed off to Oregon.

Our wedding and honeymoon were precursors of the life of faith we were soon to be embarking upon. At the last minute, Charlie's ex-business partner called to tell him that someone, who owed them money for sheep they had sold from their side business, had finally paid up. The $200.00, which was his share, was a big help for our wedding expenses.

Things were so tight that a friend who knew someone at a funeral home was able to convince the funeral worker to talk to a client about having his flowers used for a wedding when his relative's funeral was over. (I might add they were beautiful and matched the color scheme perfectly!)

Throwing a mattress and a box of groceries in the back of our station wagon, Charlie and I were off and running on our honeymoon. Sleeping in our car on cliffs overlooking the Pacific Ocean was romantic and as hokey as it may sound, I wouldn't trade the experience for anything.

Eleven days later we returned home to seven children and to the reality that we were really going to have to trust the Lord to provide for us. This was the beginning of a new and challenging life, saturated with prayer.

One day Charlie and I went shopping at the Farmer's Market where we purchased 100 lbs. of pinto beans. (We ate a lot of beans in those early days of our marriage.) We knew of a woman in our church that was struggling financially so we gave half the beans to this dear lady. Upon our return home we discovered two grocery bags full of frozen meat at our back door. This walk of faith was beginning to look quite promising.

Tithing was something I had always wanted to do and now that I was married to a devoted Christian, I was optimistic about giving God His portion of our income. Charlie wasn't quite so sure, but after seeing that God had turned our beans into meat, he was willing to try.

Charlie took a big step of faith and wrote a tithe check. I assured him that God would take care of us. Didn't the Bible say so? He gave me a big smile and agreed to go forward. This Christian life was really something different for Charlie, but we were going to trust God together. That made all the difference. We prayed after he wrote the check and then went to bed. We knew God would take care of us.

Baby Steps

The next morning, as we were getting ready to work in our little vegetable garden, we were startled when a large explosion rocked our house. We learned a railroad car of ammunitions, less than a mile from our house had caught fire and some of the contents exploded. Fortunately, no one was hurt. Many homes were damaged, including ours, but within a week the Southern Pacific Railroad had settled all claims. When all the repairs were completed, we had money left over amounting to the exact amount of one of his paychecks!

Together Charlie and I started working with a group of children in the church and life was good. Charlie's faith and faithfulness were inspiring to me and life had never seemed better. We were quite a bunch that filled a whole pew at Carmichael Bible Church.

As with any patchwork family there were ups and downs, but prayers kept being answered. We started praying the Lord would help us get a bigger house in the country. Since I had learned about praying specifically for our needs, I asked God to give us an old white farmhouse on 5-10 acres. Every single day Charlie and I bombarded Heaven for a roomy farmhouse in which to raise our kids and maybe even a few cows and goats to roam on the acreage.

One day Charlie called me from work and told me they were going to transfer his department to Georgia. He said, "How would you like to move to Georgia?" Believe me, that had never entered my mind, but at the same time I knew this would be a great new start for the Tuck family.

We immediately put our house on the market. Several months went by and there were no takers. One Sunday afternoon Charlie was leading all of us in prayer in our living room. We heard the door open, but no one dared open their eyes (not exactly protocol) and he just kept praying.

When Charlie ended the prayer with, 'Amen!' it was our signal to look up. Standing at the door was the real estate lady with a couple who had come to view the house. (It just happened to be the last day of our listing agreement with the real estate company!)

The real estate agent apologized profusely for entering without knocking, but I believe those prayers must have impressed the couple because later that day they made a good offer on the house and we were on our way to Georgia!

Traveling 3,000 miles across the country with seven children, during the 1973-74 oil embargo was a challenge. Several times we had to wait hours for a gas delivery before we could go any farther. Amazingly, with all the kids cramped into the station wagon; there were no fights or disasters except one incident.

After waiting three hours in Missouri for gas we all climbed back in the station wagon, tired but happy to be on our way. We were about ten miles down the road when the kids informed us that we had forgotten our twelve-year-old daughter Linda. Sure enough, when we did a head count, she was missing and so it was back to the gas station.

Linda always saw the bright side of things and she was patiently waiting with a big smile on her face when we returned for her. I'm still wondering, after all these years, why we went a whole ten miles down the road before the kids mentioned Linda was missing. I guess there are some things I'll never figure out.

When we arrived in Georgia, tired but relieved that the long trip was over, Charlie signed in and reported to his workplace in the gyro shop at Robins AFB. Full of faith and confidence in the Lord, he told his new co-workers that he had come from California and felt God was going to give him an old, white farmhouse on 5-10 acres. They just shook their heads in disbelief.

The very next day we started house hunting. I had discovered, after talking with several realtors, that there were no old farmhouses for sale in Warner Robins. I was not discouraged at all. I just took my Georgia map and drew a fifty-mile radius circle around the base and plotted a course for us.

The first town we went to was Hawkinsville, but nothing was available that met our criteria. We were very specific on what we believed God was going to give us. As we drove out of Hawkinsville, we saw a sign that read: *Cochran — 11 miles*. Off we went, crossing a river and a short distance up a small highway to Cochran.

Standing in the real estate office, we shared with the agent about our trek across country and told him exactly what we believed God wanted us to purchase; an old, white farmhouse on 5-10 acres.

He was very specific right back at us. There was absolutely nothing available fitting that description. While we were standing there, the phone rang. He answered and listened carefully, saying very little. Then his jaw dropped, and he shook his head in disbelief. "I can't believe this," he said. "This lady just called to list her house and it's on seven acres."

Charlie and I were ecstatic. I said, "Praise the Lord. Let's go see it!"

Mr. and Mrs. Elton Pettis owned the old, white farmhouse on 7 acres. They had told the agent they would list it on Tuesday. This was Saturday and even though the agent wasn't going to be able to show us the interior of the house; he agreed to show us the property from the road.

The old, white farmhouse was built in 1885. It was built from lumber cut from trees that, at one time, had grown on the property. He quoted the price and right there on the spot, Charlie and I told him we would take it. "But you haven't seen the inside," protested the agent.

Did we really need to see the inside? Faith doesn't have to see everything. Faith believes! When we had prayed exactly for this kind of property and it became available right when we were standing in the real estate office, we didn't have a doubt in the world that this was our house.

That was 1974. Forty-five years later we are still living on that seven-acre plot of land. Unless we see a message in the sky that reads, 'Jerri and Charlie, it's time to move' we

Everything by Prayer

won't leave this spot. Our God is truly a God who answers prayer specifically.

We were growing and our baby steps in prayer were getting bigger every day.

Chapter 5 - WE LIVE IN A ZOO

"My God shall supply all your needs according to His riches in glory by Christ Jesus."
Philippians 4:19

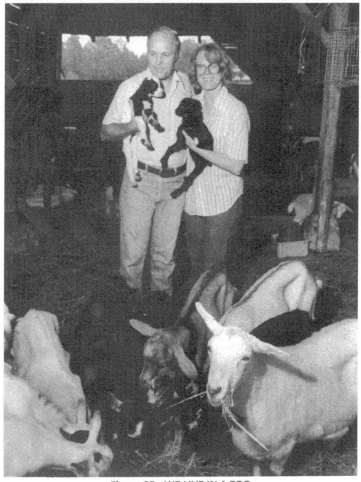

Figure 22 - WE LIVE IN A ZOO

When Charlie and I first married we had one dog and twelve chinchillas. The chinchilla episode should have tipped me off that being married to this West Virginia man was going to be an adventure.

Since our income was very small for nine of us to survive on, Charlie was always looking for ways to increase our funds. Raising chinchillas sounded like a pretty good way to earn a few extra bucks.

The problem came when one of the chinchillas bit Charlie so hard on the hand that it drew blood. Out with the chinchillas and back to the drawing board. Before Charlie could figure out another money crop of animals on our small, postage stamp-sized lot, the government came through with the transfer to Georgia. Whew!

The purchase of a farmhouse on seven acres was a dream come true for Charlie. Goodness, there was so much land he could even raise elephants if he so desired.

Elephants weren't exactly a money crop in Georgia so Charlie scoured the ads and found a place where we could buy some calves. We had only been living in Cochran a few months and since our property had some fencing and an old barn that seemed like a good plan.

We drove for about an hour to where the calves were for sale and loaded them into a borrowed trailer. Who knew it rained in July? In Sacramento it only rained in the winter. As we drove along in the pouring rain, I kept glancing through the back window of our pickup truck and looked at the 18 little critters getting soaked to the bone.

Unfortunately, half of the calves died within two weeks with pneumonia. The money we had borrowed to purchase them was going to be hard to recoup. Charlie was undaunted. Somehow, even with our losses, we managed to break even. That was the last time we tried to make money with cows.

One day I came home from the store and nearly passed out with shock. Running all around on our dining room floor were white bunny rabbits. I shrieked, "What is going on here?"

Charlie and the kids were laughing their heads off as Charlie tried to explain that we were going to make a lot of money raising rabbits. Oh, really? Not in my house!

After the initial shock we managed to corral all the critters and get them caged up and we were in the rabbit business for a few years. In fact, it wasn't long before everyone in Cochran knew where they could buy rabbits. Rabbits were easier to raise than cows and not a one died on us, in fact they multiplied like crazy!

Wanting to expand his livestock from just having rabbits Charlie said, "Honey, look at this." He was holding a Farmer's Market Bulletin newspaper and read the ad to me with some embellishment, "Goats are only $8 each. I know we can make a good profit at that price!"

His plan sounded good until I learned there was one little *catch*. You had to buy ALL of them and that meant purchasing 100 goats. "Are you serious?"

He was . . . and so we were off to a town several hours away. Homer, Georgia was not the end of the world, but I bet you could see it from your back porch. It was sure a lot farther than what we had been told by the farmer who was selling the goats. This was back in the day before you could accurately figure out distances with a GPS.

When we finally arrived at our destination it was almost dark. To top it off all the goats were running around on a fenced acre of land. The farmer said, "No problem. We'll just throw some feed in the back of your trailer and they'll hop right in!" Well . . . he was almost right. About 75 of them hopped in after the feed and then Charlie and the farmer had to catch the rest of them.

As we started for home, I got the giggles. We thought we had a lot of kids when we added up *his and mine*, but nothing compared to the load we were now carrying. As Charlie drove, I snuggled two little kids on my lap. Charlie had handed them to me through the truck window to keep them from getting trampled on.

Going through the rural area of Georgia with nearly a hundred goats, squalling in the trailer was quite the adventure . . . until we looked at the gas gauge. Our truck was close to empty with several hours of travel still ahead before we reached Cochran. We had spent every dime purchasing the goats and buying gas for the trip up to Homer. What were we going to do now? We didn't have two cents between us.

We found the nearest gas station and pulled the truck to a stop. There we prayed, while the truckload of goats said their own prayer. As we were waiting on God for help, a man came up to Charlie's window and tapped on it. "Hi Mister," he said. "Would you be willing to sell one of those goats?"

Would we? Thank you, Jesus! We were able to sell one goat which provided enough money to get enough gas to get all the way home to Cochran!

Through the succeeding years we also raised turkeys, pigs, donkeys, chickens, worms (worms for fishing) and even a ferret. Our zoo is now closed and the only animal we now have is one little Chiweenie (Chihuahua and Dachshund mix) named Moe.

When I look back at those wonderful years of the *Tuck Zoo,* I'm amazed at how God provided everything we needed to feed and take care of the animals and more than enough to raise our children.

We even made quite a decent profit on the goats. As for the rabbits, they earned their feed and more! The bonus in all of this was a lot of fun and financially we brought our credit rating up from a bankruptcy status, to a level of respectable citizens.

God has been more than good to Charlie and Jerri Tuck . . . even while living in a zoo!

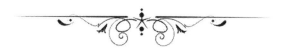

Chapter 6 - I AM THE LORD THAT HEALS YOU

"If thou wilt diligently hearken to the voice of the LORD thy God, and wilt do that which is right in His sight, and wilt give ear to His commandments, and keep all His statutes, I will put none of these diseases upon thee, which I have brought upon the Egyptians: for I am the LORD that healeth thee."
Exodus 15:26

Figure 23 - GOD DOES THE HEALING, BUT...

Shortly after moving to Georgia in 1974 we met some folks that took the Bible literally. Incredibly they believed that healing was for today and not just something that took place 2,000 years ago when Jesus walked on the earth.

I thought these people were a little bit on the fanatic side until I made a decision to get a Bible with absolutely no references and read for myself the Gospels (Matthew, Mark, Luke and John) to see if healing miracles were a thing of the past.

After a concentrated search of the Gospels and on into letters written by Apostles Paul, John, Peter and Dr. Luke, I came to a positive conclusion: God was still in the healing business! Thankfully, up to that point, I had not been tested on the authenticity of that conclusion.

Eventually my hypothesis was put to the test. It was at this juncture that Charlie had a bad fall at work, causing severe damage to his back. The pain was intense and eventually he wound up in the hospital where they performed a series of x-rays on his back.

The doctor came into the room with the results, which weren't good! "Mr. Tuck," said the doctor with a somber expression on his face, "I can operate, but the truth of the matter is, you may wind up being paralyzed."

We looked at each other and without question decided NOT to go the surgery route. When the doctor left the room I stated, "Well, we can believe the doctor's report; or we can believe God's report for healing."

Leaving the hospital in no better condition than when we had arrived, we were a bit discouraged, but we both started agreeing and praying for God to heal his back. Instead of healing, the pain seemed to grow worse.

I remembered the story Jesus told in Matthew 13 where the farmer sowed seed into the ground and the fowls of the air came to steal the seed just as soon as it was sown. I had only recently received the seed on healing and the devil was doing his best to steal it from my heart, but I wouldn't let him.

Each day we claimed healing. Each day the pain grew worse. One day Charlie received a call from a friend asking him to help with some plumbing at our church. They were going to have to crawl under a trailer to fix some leaking pipes.

I was adamant that he shouldn't go because of all the pain he was going through with his back. He was just as adamant that his friend needed his help; so off he went.

A few hours later I saw him driving up the driveway and I flew out the door to help him out of the car. Before I could get to him, he was on the sidewalk doing jumping jacks! "What are you doing?" I yelled.

Laughing, he answered, "God healed me!"

I was laughing too and said, "Stop before you get unhealed!"

We both rejoiced in what God had done for Charlie under that trailer. More than the healing of his lower back (in which the pain has never returned), was the knowledge that God's Word is truth! He is the Lord (Jehovah Rapha) that heals!

In 1990, at age 50, I went through my own test in believing God for healing. For several days I was experiencing stomach pain. Finally, I made an appointment to see Dr. Ed Roberts, our local physician.

As Dr. Roberts performed a sonogram on my stomach he pointed to the machine and said, "Do you see that mass?" Bigger than life was a huge black blob on the screen, which I was informed was the *mass*. Of course, when we hear the word *mass*, we naturally think of cancer.

The doctor then called for the nurse to come into the room and told her to make an appointment with a specialist in Macon. When she returned and said it would be several weeks before he could see me, he yelled at her, "I want her in TOMORROW!"

His fierceness in answering the nurse in that way caused me some alarm. Could I have cancer?

Remembering what God had done for Charlie with his back and what I had been learning about healing from the Word of God, I refused to give in to fear.

That night I had a very long talk with the Lord. In fact, I don't think I slept all night. My conversation went something like this: "Okay, God. You and I both believe in healing and I don't need to get down to 86 pounds like Dodie Osteen did to prove that You are the healer. Whatever it is, I believe it will be gone."

I had just finished a book about Dodie, *Healed of Cancer*, where she shared that she had received an awful report about having liver cancer. In 1981 the doctors told her she had only weeks to live. Dodie was a firm believer in healing and although she dropped to 86 lbs., she beat cancer; infact, is still alive 38 years later!

The next day I stopped by our office to tell my husband I was on the way to the doctor. (I hadn't told him about the mass, as I didn't want to worry him or to hear any possible words that might possibly shake my faith.) It just so happened that our pastor was in the office visiting with Charlie that day.

Pastor Steve Moore said, "Can I say a prayer for you before you head up to Macon?"

I told him that would be nice.

"What shall we pray for . . ." he asked, ". . . a good report?"

"That would work," I told him. Then he gently laid his hand on my shoulder and said:

"Lord, we just believe that Jerri will get a good report at the doctor's office today."

So simple . . . but believing IS simple. Anyone can believe. Jesus said we were to have the faith of a child.

When the second sonogram was done in Macon the mass was completely gone, as was all the stomach pain.

Through these years we have had other miraculous healings, as well as surgical and medicinal healings. We are of the opinion that whatever vehicle God decides to use is good with us. Sometimes our faith has wavered a bit, and other times we have been bold as a lion in believing for healing. Hanging from the wall of one of our doctors was a sign that said, "God does the healing, but the doctor collects the fee." That just about sums it up for us as far as doctors and medicine goes.

Sometimes it seems as if God just allows certain things to come against us so we can tell the world that God is a healer. There is no doubt in my mind that we must take an active approach against sickness and diseases with the Word of God.

As a last testimony on God's amazing healing I'll share one more account. About ten years ago I had a headache which really knocked me for a loop. Since I rarely have headaches, I was surprised, but took an aspirin and the headache disappeared.

The next day at church the headache started again. I told my husband I would never be able to make it through the service because my head was hurting so badly. I asked him if he would mind catching a ride home with someone because I was leaving.

As I drove away from the church my head was pounding and instead of going home, I decided to go straight to the hospital. By the time I arrived I was in extreme pain. They immediately gave me something for pain and I settled down. After 30 minutes or so I realized that no one knew where I was, so I called one of our daughters.

Sandy, who is a Registered Nurse, was quite alarmed when she learned my symptoms and had them do an MRI to make sure I wasn't having a stroke. As it turned out I had a case of Shingles.

I went home, heavily medicated with pain medicine, and went to sleep. That night the Lord woke me up and spoke to my heart, "Just as I have decreed that the waves should go just so far and no farther, I decree that these shingles will go no farther."

I went back to sleep in total peace that I had heard God's word on my healing. The next morning my husband, who had slept in another room, so as not to bother me, came in. I said, "Honey, get a chair and sit by me and read the Bible to me."

Over 30,000 verses in the Bible and he randomly opened it and began to read, *"'Do you not fear me?' declares the LORD. 'Do you not tremble in My presence? For I have placed the sand as a boundary for the sea, an eternal limit, and it will not cross over it. Though the waves toss, they cannot prevail; though they roar, they will not cross over it.'"* (Jeremiah 5:22 NASB)

It was the exact same verse God gave me the night before!

I think I may have had the mildest case of Shingles in history. From that point on the pain was gone and I had another testimony about our healing God! Friend, you can choose to believe God is still healing today, or you can just give up. What's your choice?

Chapter 7 - A TISKET, A TASKET

"Now unto Him that is able to do exceedingly abundantly above all that we ask or think, according to the power that worketh in us, Unto Him be glory in the church by Christ Jesus throughout all ages, world without end. Amen."
Ephesians 3:20-21

Figure 24 - EASTER BASKETS

One of the things I faced as a stepmom was trying to make both of our little ones feel equally loved. When we married in 1972 Charlie's youngest daughter was two years old and my youngest daughter was only one year old.

With just eight months between them age-wise, they felt like twins. Virginia's mom lived 3,000 miles away in California, but she was always faithful in sending cards for various occasions. To make Dotty, the youngest, feel equally loved and thought about, I would make sure she received cards too.

During one particularly hard financial time we were attending a little Baptist church and they began their plans for an annual Easter egg hunt. Each child was to bring his or her own Easter basket.

I know that sounds like a small thing, but when your husband has been out of work for months because of a surgery and you've been forced to go on food stamps, an Easter basket looked like an insurmountable expense for which there was no money available.

To make matters worse, Virginia's mother had sent her an Easter dress, complete with a hat, gloves and a little purse. I was distraught to say the least.

At the same time the package arrived with Virginia's presents, our son Jeff received an Easter card from his birth mom. I had no idea what was in his card until our older girls informed me that Jeff had received $5 and to top it off, they told me he had no intention of telling me about the money!

What do you do at a time like that? Well, I'll tell you what I did. I prayed saying, "Lord, please tell Jeff to give me that money and when we get our Workman's Compensation money (they were behind on 30,000 cases!) I'll give him double the money back so he will learn he can't out give you!"

I went outside to hang out my laundry on the clothesline and it seemed like that old devil went to work overtime! He whispered in my ear, "Are you kidding? Jeff isn't going to give you that money."

I yelled, "Yes, he is devil! And you just leave him and me alone right now in the mighty name of Jesus!" Ha! He backed off and I began singing and praising God for what I knew He was going to do.

Finishing up my laundry task I went into the house and Jeff came to me and said, "Mom, my mom in California sent me $5 in my Easter card and I want you to have it." I just started crying.

"Jeff, when daddy gets his money back from Workmen's Compensation, I'm going to give you back double so you will know you can't out give God." Jeff didn't want the money back because he wanted to help, but you can bet I gave him back $10 when our money came in a few months later.

At that period in our lives Charlie had just started back to work and I was making a whopping $200 a month writing for the Macon Telegraph and News as a feature writer and reporter. Money was more than tight.

That particular day I sent Charlie off to work with $1 for coffee money, gave $1 to a friend who was going through a tough time financially, and put $3 in the gas tank so I could make it out of town to do my newspaper assignment.

On the way home, I had those Easter baskets on my mind. The Easter egg hunt was the next day and I had no money. I stopped at a drugstore and went in, determined to do something myself about the dilemma I was in. "I'm going to buy those girls Easter baskets." I said to myself: "If my check bounces, it bounces!"

As I reached for the $1.27 Easter baskets, I heard the voice of the Lord in my spirit, "If you touch those Easter baskets, I'll not give you good ones." I quickly drew my hand back as if I had been burned by a hot iron. Heading to my car I said, "Okay, Lord. No one knows we need Easter baskets but You, so I am trusting in You!"

Later that evening Jeff came into my bedroom with a downcast look. "Mom, I was really hoping you would buy Easter baskets for Virginia and Dotty with the five dollars I gave to you."

"Jeff, don't you remember God providing the money we needed for our electric bill? What are two little Easter baskets to such a mighty prayer answering God? Let's get down on our knees and pray together about those baskets." We did and God heard!

The next morning before we got out of bed the phone rang and a stranger said, "Mrs. Tuck, someone just called me and asked me to call and see if you could possibly use two Easter baskets."

I guess you know my answer on that one. "Can I bring them by at one o'clock?" she added.

Since the Easter egg hunt was taking place at 2 p.m. the timing couldn't have been more perfect. At one o'clock the lady brought two, huge Easter baskets brimming with everything from candy to sunglasses. In addition, she brought a cake and an Easter card which contained $25.

After I dropped our happy little preschoolers off at the church, toting their huge Easter baskets, I headed straight to the fabric store. Easter was the next day and I had a dress to sew for Dotty.

I was a bit bleary-eyed in church on Easter morning, after sewing all night long, but I was sure a happy momma looking at our little girls all dressed up so fancy in their polka-dotted Swiss dresses. Virginia's was lavender and Dotty's dress was pink and looked identical except for the color.

To top that off, there was enough money left over after purchasing the material that I was able to buy a hat, gloves and a little purse for Dotty. No wonder they thought they were twins growing up and no wonder I believe in prayer!

Chapter 8 - THE BLESSING OF GOD'S WORD

"Forever O Lord, thy word is settled in Heaven."
Psalm 119:89

Figure 25 - COURTHOUSE & THE BIBLE READING MARATHON

I was intrigued by an article I read in a small devotional book entitled, Bible Pathway. According to the article, Bible Pathway founder Dr. John Hash, along with Dr. Bill Bright of Campus Crusade for Christ got together and conducted a Bible Reading Marathon on the steps of our nation's capital in 1990.

This baby step of faith, beginning in 1990 has been spreading throughout the United States and to other parts of the world. I began to think that maybe we could get one started in Cochran, Georgia.

I had no idea how to organize something like this. However, since they offered a *How to Kit*, I sent for one and waited anxiously for it to arrive. Was I in for a surprise! Reading the material, I realized this was no small task. I felt totally unqualified to attempt something of such magnitude for our little town. I promptly threw the book into the trash can. "Maybe someone else, Lord, but not me!"

About three months passed and the Lord started speaking to my heart again about organizing a Bible Reading Marathon in our little town. I had been reading in Ezra about God stirring up the spirit of King Cyrus to help the Jews return to Jerusalem and somehow that spoke to me. "Lord, stir the hearts of the pastors in our town if this is something that You want done here in Cochran."

I had been praying regularly for about three weeks when a local pastor called to discuss a house I had for sale. After going over the details of the property and setting up an appointment to show him the house; I hesitantly asked, "Pastor, what do you think about our town holding a Bible Reading Marathon?"

I quickly explained about the organization that had been doing this and how the marathons were spreading in other states and whether he thought Cochran could do something like this. I was amazed when he thought it was a great idea.

The next day when I met him to show him the house which was for sale, he informed me that he had spoken to the president of the local ministerial alliance and that he would like to meet me to discuss this project.

I was ecstatic and yet a bit nervous at the same time. I had never met Pastor Hutchings and I wasn't quite sure how he would receive me, since I wasn't a member of his denomination. Believing I was on the right track about this project; I called the church and made an appointment to discuss the marathon with him.

The night before I was to meet with the pastor, the Lord awakened me about 2 a.m. and told me to go my computer. Wiping the sleep out of my eyes I headed to my study. As I sat staring bleary-eyed at the blank screen I said, "Okay Lord, now what?"

Suddenly, I was wide awake as the Lord spoke to my heart, "The pastor is going to have five objections. Here's what they are and here is the rebuttal."

My fingers flew over the keys as I wrote what the Lord was instructing. When I finished typing I printed out the objections and answers, put them into a manila folder and went back to bed.

The next day I headed to the church. Seated at a table in the fellowship hall, arms folded tightly against his chest, was the pastor. I introduced myself and took a seat, wondering just where this was all going.

"Well," said the pastor without a hint of a smile, "I understand you want to have a Bible Reading Marathon here in Cochran. I'm just wondering about. . . . ." You guessed it. He reiterated the exact five objections.

I slid the manila folder across the table and with an astonished look on his face he read the questions and answers. Shutting the folder, he smiled and said, "When do we begin?"

That was 2004 when an amazing adventure began in our community, as Christians from nearly every denomination began to work together in partnership to read God's Word during one special week each year from the steps of our Bleckley County Courthouse.

There have been some trials along the way, but prayer and the declaration of God's Word and His victory have taken us over every hurdle.

After I got the go ahead from the local ministerial alliance the work began. I learned later that the county commissioner thought I was crazy and thinking it would probably never work; he granted permission to hold the marathon at the courthouse.

With 90 hours of reading to complete the entire Bible from Genesis to Revelation I was going to need a lot of help. When I shared the vision with my Sunday school class everyone smiled and thought it was a great idea, but no one volunteered to read.

Everything by Prayer

I was discouraged but undaunted. I told God if it was just Him and me I would do it even if I had to hit *play* on my cassette recorder. I was determined.

Shortly after I told the Lord that I would do the marathon, even if I had to do it by myself, the phone rang. A young woman, who had been good friends with our two youngest daughters while they were in high school, told me she had read the letters I had sent to her father and brother, who were both pastors.

Figure 26 - 4-27-07 - PRESCHOOL CHOIR AT BRM

She said she wanted to read in the marathon. I was ecstatic! With pen in hand ready to write her name down as our first reader I said, "That's wonderful Cynthia. What 15 minutes would you like to read?"

"Ms. Tuck you don't understand. I want to read the Bible for five hours. I just became a Christian and I'm really into reading the Bible." Not only was I floored, I started crying. I had prayed for this young lady's salvation for years and now here she was, not only telling me she was a Christian, but that

The Blessing of God's Word

she wanted to read the Bible for five hours! Only God could do such a wonderful, amazing and encouraging thing.

The Lord assured me from that point on I would never have to worry about getting readers to fill the schedule. He was behind this whole endeavor and when He blesses something, it is blessed indeed! That was the beginning of 16 years of miracles with readers having always filled every minute of every hour. When you do the math it's absolutely astounding. This comes to 1,440 hours (16 years x 90 hours) of Bible reading from the steps of our courthouse.

As the day approached for the start of the first Bible Reading Marathon in the state of Georgia, I had an idea. The night before the opening ceremony I called the president of the ministerial alliance and said, "Pastor, I think God wants us to meet at 8 a.m. at the courthouse, before it opens, and walk around it seven times." (Joshua 6:10)

By this time the pastor was on board all the way. "Who do you want me to invite?" I told him anyone he wanted to invite was fine with me.

The next morning, as I was getting ready to go into town, I had another thought. "It sure would be neat to have small white rocks, a size that would fit in the palm of the hand. We could place them in front of the courthouse, tucked away in a secluded corner as a testimony, so that even when we're not reading the Bible the rocks will be crying out praises to God." (Luke 19:40)

I immediately called both daughters who live in Cochran and neither one had any rocks. Around 7:30 a.m. a friend called out of the blue; she had never called me that early before. In the course of our conversation I told her what was going on and asked her if she had any rocks. She said, "Hey, as a matter of fact I just bought some for Vacation Bible School. I'll meet you down at the courthouse!"

As I drove to the courthouse, I was rejoicing about the rocks. I had this thought, "Wouldn't it be neat if there were twelve of us, since each one of the twelve tribes of Israel set up rocks by the Jordan River as a testimony to generations to come?"

Figure 27 - PASTOR HUTCHINGS - EMCEE - 2004 BRM

When I drove into the parking lot there were eight people gathered; counting my husband and me we had ten. Then suddenly, walking around to the back of the courthouse where we had gathered was one of my daughters and her pastor's wife. We had our twelve! Way to go, God!

Quickly, after going over what we were going to be doing, the pastor led us in a prayer, and we started our first trek around the courthouse. We were quite a sight in the light drizzling rain. The pastor led the way, holding an umbrella. Charlie and I followed right behind him under an umbrella and everyone else followed with umbrellas and rocks in hand.

We had just finished one round when the county commissioner arrived in his pickup truck. He lowered his window and dryly asked the pastor, "Going for a walk?"

The pastor told him, "Yes."

The commissioner rolled his eyes and said, "Have a good one!" and promptly parked his truck and went into the courthouse.

By the time we finished our seventh time around the courthouse, all the county employees were looking out the windows at the crazy people walking around and around; but instead of being intimidated we gained more boldness.

Figure 28 - GEORGIA STATE SENATOR ROSS TOLLISON AT BRM

After saying a prayer over the courthouse and the rocks the pastor, who by this time had become just as fanatic as Jerri

Everything by Prayer

Tuck, said, "I think we all need to go out to the front sidewalk and yell praises to God at the courthouse."

So . . . there we were. Twelve of us, from young to old, from various churches and denominations yelling, "PRAISE GOD! HALLELUJAH! JESUS IS LORD! THE VICTORY IS GOD'S!"

With hugs and spiritual high fives, we all drove away from the courthouse and headed home, praising God and anxious for 6 p.m. to arrive and the first Bible Reading Marathon in Georgia to begin.

In 2019 we held our 16th Annual Bible Reading Marathon and I was just as excited about it then as I was that very first year. Something happens in a community when the Word of God is honored. To begin with, God is pleased and with His pleasure comes blessing.

His Word tells us that those who honor Him, He in turn will honor. We are a blessed community. There is visible unity in our community because of this Bible Reading Marathon. Some may have differing views on modes of baptism, we may differ in styles of worship and have various views on prophetic happenings, but we all agree that God's Word is the best guidebook for life here and to prepare us for the life to come!

Chapter 9 - WHEN PRAYERS CONNECT

"So Cornelius said, 'Four days ago I was fasting until this hour; and at the ninth hour I prayed in my house, and behold, a man stood before me in bright clothing, and said, 'Cornelius, your prayer has been heard, and your alms are remembered in the sight of God.'"
Acts 10:30-31

Figure 29 - HOME BIBLE STUDY MIDDLE GEORGIA COLLEGE

Watching our little girls play by the huge college pond was a good time of prayer and reflection for me each school day. We had a little routine that had provided fun and enjoyment for Dotty and Virginia and a quiet time for me as I would pray concerning a ministry to college students.

After the older children were off to school, I would take the youngest two children to our local college and watch them as they played, all the while praying for an open door to share the gospel with the college students.

Prayer is not always being on one's knees with eyes shut. Most of my praying, especially when the children were young, was standing at a kitchen sink washing dishes, or hanging clothes on a clothesline. I learned early on that it wasn't my physical position, but the condition of my heart in relationship to God.

As I have grown in my Christian life, I've learned another thing about prayer that is pretty mind boggling. Prayer is more than just a two-way street – not just you talking to God and Him talking to you. Many times, prayer is a three or four-way or even *more* proposition. Sometimes you are the one who literally becomes an answer to someone else's prayer!

In one of the college dorms there was a group of college students that were very zealous for the Lord. Glenn and David were in this group and had begun praying earnestly that a home would somehow be provided where they could take their friends and in the relaxed atmosphere of a home, they could share the truths of God's word.

College life is fun and crazy at times, but there's nothing like a good old-fashioned home with a mom and pop and times of refreshment to take your mind off your studies.

David Koto was a very zealous young man who had a burning zeal to win others to faith in Christ . . . even when the prospects were just children.

One day our 13-year-old daughter Linda was playing at the Bleckley Middle School just a short distance from our home and David, the college evangelist, came up to her and started talking to her about Jesus. In the process he gave her a gospel tract and told her to be sure and read the story contained therein.

Linda hopped on her bicycle and raced home with the tract in her hand. Linda knew we had been praying for the college students and she was ecstatic about meeting David. Maybe this was the beginning of something to bring those prayers to fruition.

When I asked her if the young man was still down at the school, she told me he had gone back to the college. "If you ever see him again, you hop right back on that bike and

When Prayers Connect

hurry home," I told her. I began to pray even harder for the students at the college.

Several weeks later Linda, who was breathless, jumped off her bike and ran into the house. "He's down at the school again, Mom. If you want to meet him, you better hurry."

Not caring what I looked like, I jumped into my car and headed for the school. I must have looked like a crazy old woman with my head covered in huge curlers and not a touch of makeup! I'm so glad David looked past the outward and that day, at the Bleckley County Middle School, our hearts were knit together.

David and Glenn and several other students had been praying for a home in which to meet and I had been praying for the college students. It was a perfect fit and one which would continue year after year. Even today, 45+ years later, I am still in contact with some of these students. What a blessing!

Prayers at times can be connected in mysterious ways. One summer day, as I was driving out of town, I neared the top of a hill and distinctly heard the voice of the Lord telling me to turn left onto a little dirt drive. I had been earnestly praying that day as I was driving and so, without a second's hesitation, I made the turn.

As I came upon a little rise, a Civil War cemetery came into view. It was obscured by some very tall pine trees. I had never been down this road before and so of course, I had no idea there was a cemetery there.

Surrounding the cemetery was an old stone wall about three feet high. Curious, I opened the creaky wrought iron gate and entered the small cemetery. Still in a prayerful state, I sat down on a concrete slab and continued praying. The fellowship with the Lord just became so real that I decided to get down on my knees and really get in touch with the Lord! I have no idea how long I had been praying (or how loud), but I suddenly had the feeling someone was watching me.

Figure 30 - CIVIL WAR CEMETRY - MACON-COCHRAN HWY

I looked up as a man entered the cemetery. I was busted! I couldn't very well say I was just looking at the dates on the tombstones. I didn't know what else to say but, "Hi. This just looked like a good place to pray."

The man introduced himself and I told him who I was; he grunted out that he knew who I was because he had read my news articles in the Macon Telegraph. (Whew! At least he knew I wasn't a grave robber!)

In a flash, God's voice came to my spirit saying, "This is why I led you into this cemetery. I want you to tell this man how to be saved." Friend, that was incredible. My detour down the dirt road had a bigger purpose than I had realized.

Many days later I was sharing my experience with a friend and she blew me away when she said, "Oh, Jerri. We have been praying that God would lead someone to tell him how to be saved!"

In more recent times I was on a trip to Nigeria where I met a young man who was far away from God. Before the week ended, he had made a 180 degree turn and recommitted his life to the Lord. Was that all Jerri Tuck? Not a chance. A big church family had been praying for this young man and God heard them and sent me all the way from America to let this young man know that God loved him and cared deeply about him.

Friend, when you pray, God is listening, and He cares. You may be the answer to someone else's prayer, while someone else may be an answer to your prayer. Prayers connect and God gets all the glory.

"Who then is Paul, and who is Apollos, but ministers through whom you believed, as the Lord gave to each one. I planted, Apollos watered, but God gave the increase. So then neither he who plants is anything, nor he who waters, but God who gives the increase" (I Corinthians 3:5-7).

Chapter 10 - GOD CAN CHANGE THE GOVERNMENT

"Therefore I exhort first of all that supplications, prayers, intercessions, and giving of thanks be made for all men, for kings and all who are in authority, that we may lead a quiet and peaceable life in all godliness and reverence; for this is good and acceptable in the sight of God our Savior, who desires all men to be saved and to come to the knowledge of the truth."
I Timothy 2:1-4 (NKJV)

Figure 31 - DOTTY & VIRGINIA IN THEIR YOUNGER DAYS

When we arrived in Georgia in 1974, I was very ignorant about the workings of government. For instance, I didn't realize that integration of the schools was only a few years old and Bleckley County, although having had a pretty smooth transition, was still fraught with discrimination.

Coming from a fully integrated society I had no idea that any of those social issues were problematic, however I was facing a different problem with the school situation.

Everything by Prayer

In combining our two families, Charlie's youngest child and my youngest child were very close in age. With just eight months separating them I was dreading the start of kindergarten. According to the rules set by the State of Georgia a child had to be five years old by September 1st before entering kindergarten.

Virginia, Charlie's youngest, had turned five years old in March, but Dotty, my youngest, wouldn't hit the magic age until the end of November. This was a huge problem because the girls did everything together. In their minds they were twins, although they didn't resemble each other in the least!

Before 1975 arrived, I began praying about the situation. I knew this was going to be a serious problem in our household. Virginia was entirely too smart to hold her back, and Dotty was going to be devastated to see her 'twin' sister going to school without her.

In January of 1975 Governor George Busbee was sworn into office. Busbee, a Democrat, had formerly served nine terms in the Georgia House of Representatives and was floor leader for Governor Carl Sanders. He was one of thirty Democrats in the legislature who voted for a Republican in a 1966 gubernatorial race, rather than vote for Lester Maddox a segregationist from Atlanta.

None of this was known to me at the time. I just knew I served a great God in Heaven and knew He heard my prayers.

To this day I don't know why (other than prayer) the governor decided to change the date for starting kindergarten from September 1 to December 31. I do know there was quite a bit of rejoicing in the Tuck household when we got the word. The following year the dates for starting kindergarten were changed back to September 1.

In 2015 the Georgia House passed a bill establishing the age requirement for children enrolling in kindergarten to August 1 and in the 2018-19 term the age requirement was set to be five years old by July 1st.

God Can Change the Government

As I look back to that incredible answer to my prayers in 1974-1975, I rejoice that God worked this out better than I ever could. I had no idea that my prayer would move the Georgia governor to change the date.

When we pray, we must leave the 'how to' to our Heavenly Father. He can always do above all we could ask or think. (Ephesians 3:20)

From that fledgling prayer I became emboldened to pray about things political. I realize now that we, as Christians, don't need to drop off the planet concerning governmental affairs.

Years ago, Christians were accused of 'being so Heavenly minded they were no earthly good' and I certainly agree. Where were we Christians when prayers were taken out of public school and when the Bible became a forbidden book?

The facts are that on June 17, 1963 "school-sponsored" prayer and Bible reading was banned from public schools. It has only been in recent years that there has been a resurrection of prayer in our public schools as STUDENTS lead the charge.

In our little town we are blessed to have students organize and participate in a PRAYER WALK. Meeting on the Sunday night before school begins; the community is invited to the opening ceremony, which is held in one of the school's gyms. Collective prayers are sent up to God for students and staff and then everyone is encouraged to go to the various schools to pray.

What a beautiful sight to walk up and down the school hallways and see groups of people praying at various classroom doors. Some of the teachers even put prayer requests on their doors so people will know specifically what to pray for.

In 2016 another amazing thing happened in Cochran. We had a school superintendent who was not only a wonderful educator and a Christian, he was also very cognizant of politics and law.

Steve J. Smith, the Bleckley County School Superintendent, invited about thirty people to the school for a breakfast. I was one of those he invited. At this breakfast he informed us that we were going to be starting a Christian Learning Center. Students were going to be able to choose to take Bible courses in our school system. We were stunned!

Mr. Smith had been working in another Georgia county where this was going on and he felt strongly that this would work in Bleckley County.

In 1952 a case (Zorach v. Clauson) came before the U.S. Supreme Court involving an education law in New York State. This case was about a regulation by which a public school was permitted to release students during school hours for religious instruction or devotional exercises. The high court ruled 6 to 3 in favor of the New York law.

Figure 32 - DOTTY AND VIRGINIA GROWN UP

Mr. Smith knew this law and saw it work in a practical way with students in Wilcox County. We were asked if we would like to join him in incorporating a Christian Learning Center in Bleckley County? Every one of us who attended that first meeting agreed that this would be a wonderful thing to have in our county. I was blessed to be asked to be a member of the newly formed BCLC board.

In 2016 Bible classes began in our school system. The Lord had moved the highest court in the land to pave the way for the Bible to get back into our school systems. Since that time, we have expanded the program into two neighboring counties, Telfair and Dodge.

The latest statistics on release time participation in the United States are so encouraging. There are approximately 1,000 programs in operation, ranging from kindergarten to high school with approximately 250,000 students enrolled. In our county we have 114 children taking the Bible classes in the middle and high school age groups.

As for the prejudice that was rife when we moved to Georgia, we have seen incredible changes. Not only are all races learning together in schools, but also worshipping together in many of our churches.

Martin Luther King, Jr. was known for leading marches and protests, but he and millions of others prayed for the laws to change concerning segregation and it happened! Now we see our God changing hearts as well.

During our years of holding home Bible studies with college and high school students we not only had students attending from different racial backgrounds, but also many who were of diverse nationalities from all over the world!

Prayer changes things . . . even our government!

Chapter 11 - FROM MESS TO MESSAGE

"He brought me up also out of a horrible pit, out of the miry clay, and set my feet upon a rock, and established my goings. And he hath put a new song in my mouth, even praise unto our God: many shall see it, and fear, and shall trust in the LORD."
Psalms 40:2-3

Figure 33 - THE TUCK'S NEW HOME

Walking out of the attorney's office on that cold wintry day in 1973 was difficult at best. Charlie had just filed for bankruptcy and as we walked toward our car, I was so aware of his pain. His head was bent down and his shoulders were slumped over. His hands were stuffed in the pockets of his overcoat and he looked totally defeated. Neither of us said a word and my heart was breaking for him.

There was nothing I could say that would soften the blow of this financial setback. Seven years loomed ahead of us before the bankruptcy would be wiped off his credit and that put us in a very difficult place as we had been looking for a larger home.

Our 1200 square foot home in suburban Sacramento was quite cramped with seven children. Charlie's oldest child was out on her own when we married in September of 1972 and so, with his four and my three, we had a pretty good-sized family for the small dwelling in which we lived.

A month prior to getting married Charlie had moved in with good friends, Jim and Anita Crane. The purpose of this move was to save money for our upcoming wedding.

Charlie had moved his few meager belongings into my garage and when I asked him if he wanted me to clean out the dresser drawers for him; he was more than happy to turn the project over to me.

Organization was not one of Charlie's virtues. As I began to clean out the drawers, I discovered something else about the man I was about to marry. He was not organized with his finances either! In his top dresser drawer were dozens of bank statements that had never been opened.

When Charlie and I married in 1972 he had only been a Christian for five months. Prior to his conversion he was doing his best just to survive. A broken marriage, a habit of alcoholism and four children to take care of was almost more than he could handle.

The Bible tells us that when a person becomes a Christian, he becomes a new creation in Christ, but sometimes, as in the case of Lazarus (John 11), the old grave clothes of our previous life are still hanging on. The next time I saw Charlie I casually mentioned the bank statements and he just grinned and said, "Bookkeeping has never been my strong point." I let the matter drop and continued cleaning and working toward our wedding day.

Until the day of the bankruptcy filing, I hadn't given those bank statements a second thought. Charlie had just turned the finances all over to me and with God's help and provisions we were making it just fine. Now, with the bankruptcy looming over us, the prospects of getting a larger house were shrinking greatly.

From Mess to Message

A year later we were on our way to Georgia to begin a whole new life. The government transferred all work on gyros to Robins Air Force Base and Charlie, along with others in his department, were making the long trip across the country.

After 50 some hours of traveling in our Ford station wagon, we safely arrived in Warner Robins. By this time the bankruptcy was an old memory that we had left in California. This was a brand-new beginning for us, and we were all excited about the prospects of finding an old white farmhouse on 5-10 acres.

Charlie reported into work at Robins Air Force Base on the day we arrived in Georgia and boldly told his co-workers that God was going to give us an old white farmhouse on 5-10 acres. There were those who thought he was crazy in the head for making such a bold statement, but they were to find out that God was honoring Charlie's faith.

Indeed, God had the perfect house, just waiting for us. There was no doubt in our minds that God had led us to Cochran and to that old farmhouse. Armed with that knowledge, we sat down in front of the realtor's desk, ready to begin the loan application process.

We sat there as Danny asked question after question, filling out the loan application. Then the inevitable question came: "Have you ever had a bankruptcy?"

Taking a deep breath, Charlie answered that he had filed for bankruptcy about a year and a half ago. Danny quietly laid down his pen and said, "Tell me about it."

After Charlie finished telling him about his life before Christ and the things that had led up to him filing for bankruptcy, Danny answered, "I just won't fill in that blank."

There is no way to explain our joy and amazement at Danny's reaction and subsequent decision to leave the square blank on the loan application. It was over forty years later that I discovered the president of the savings and loan institution had no idea that Danny had done that. Apparently, God had blinded his eyes to the omission and approved our big loan of $16,000.

I was so proud of my husband for being truthful. Charlie had been growing in his new-found faith in Christ and had been learning valuable lessons in putting God first in everything. He had become a faithful giver to the work of the Lord, as well as a man who prayed before he did anything. I just knew that the Lord was honoring his faith and integrity and that we were on the brink of some fantastic blessings in this new adventure.

While we were waiting for the loan to be processed, we moved into a little single-wide trailer on the south end of Cochran. Charlie reported into work that following Monday morning and told his friends that God had provided a big old farmhouse on nearly seven acres. There were a lot of jaws dropping that Monday morning because Charlie had told them God was going to do this for us. Talk about faith!

We closed on the property within six weeks and today, over 45 years later, we are still enjoying the old house and so are many others. Today, when you drive by our plot of land, you will see two houses on our patch of land.

We're not in the old house anymore. In 2010 one of our precious children decided mom and dad needed a newer house, one that would be more comfortable in their old age. Frankly, I thought we were quite comfortable, but God's ways are not our ways and God was up to something.

To begin with, I never understood why the old farmhouse wasn't situated in the middle of the property like I had envisioned, but God had a better plan and He used our children to bring His plan into fruition.

After many months of cajoling and encouraging, our children were finally able to convince us to move into a new house and by doing so, we could use the old house to bless others.

Today visiting preachers, missionaries, singing groups and other Christians who are just traveling through the Middle Georgia area, are our welcome guests.

If walls could talk! In answer to our prayers God gave us the desire of our hearts . . . and more! We spent many happy days in that old farmhouse raising our wonderful children. Yes, there were times of trial, but many more were the times of rejoicing! We are blessed to be able to share the old home with others, at no cost to them, and we are now able to tell them how God can take our messes and turn them into messages for Him!

Figure 34 - WILSON & CORA - PHILIPPINE MISSIONARIES AT OLD HOUSE

Chapter 12 - LEARNING TO USE WISDOM

"And all things, whatsoever ye shall ask in prayer, believing, ye shall receive." Matthew 21:22

Figure 35 - JERRI'S SCOFIELD REFERENCE BIBLE

I had no idea that I was following my Grandma Krieger's footsteps when I picked up hitchhikers, only Grandma was the hitchhiker!

Back in South Dakota, Grandma who was a preacher of sorts; would stick out her thumb until a kind-hearted motorist would pick her up and give her a ride. Smiling gratefully, as she seated herself in whatever vehicle was offered, she would then proceed to tell the driver about Jesus.

As soon as Grandma decided her benefactors got the message, she would politely ask to be let off and then go to the opposite side of the road and hitchhike a ride back home, all the while sharing the message of salvation with other unsuspecting passengers.

Everything by Prayer

I, on the other hand, was the driver who picked hitchhikers up and would tell my captive audience about Jesus, many times bringing them home for a meal or snack and then take them, if possible, to their destination. I would be sure to give them some Christian literature to take on their way.

The last hitchhiker I brought home turned out to be A.W.O.L. from the military and that's when Charlie put his foot down. No more hitchhikers! Period!

The incident happened around the same time in 1978, when a 15-year-old young woman in the Sacramento area was hitchhiking. She was given a ride by a 50-year-old, ex-merchant mariner who, after he raped her, cut off her forearms with a hatchet and stuffed her in a concrete culvert to hide her body. Somehow the woman lived; but her life would never be the same.

To be truthful the A.W.O.L. person didn't frighten me, but the story about the young woman who had lost her hands and forearms certainly made an impression. I agreed with Charlie. No more picking up hitchhikers ... period!

Several months had gone by after this decision had been made when I saw a couple of young men hitchhiking. I couldn't resist and so I stopped to ask them where they were going. When they said they were headed for Savannah I promptly told them they would never get a ride at this time of night going all that distance ... especially not from Cochran, which was 20 miles from an Interstate and then another 3 hours down I-16. No way!

I went to the pay phone and called home. You guessed it! Charlie was adamant with his answer. "NO! You cannot bring them home."

"Okay guys," I said. "My husband says I can't bring you home, but you wait right here, and I'll be right back."

I jumped in my car and headed for my friend's house and told her the situation. I didn't have any money for a motel, but when Eleanor Mathews, my good friend and mentor, heard the story she gave me enough money for the young men to obtain a motel room. Delighted, I headed back to the spot where the young men were waiting.

They were shocked to see me return and were still trying to hitch a ride, but just like I had told them; there was no way, especially at night in Cochran, that they would be able to catch a ride to Savannah.

Resisting the urge to give them a ride, I told them exactly where the motel was located, in fact it was only about a mile from where they were presently trying to get a ride. I gave them the money and when I looked in my pocketbook for a Christian tract, I discovered I was completely out!

Since I always carried my Bible with me, I handed it to them and told them to read everything I had underlined (which was a bunch). Their mouths dropped open. The money was one thing, but they certainly didn't expect a Bible to boot!

"We can't take your Bible, Ma'am," they protested.

I insisted and that was that! Waving goodbye to them I headed on home, satisfied they would find a ride the next day.

Three weeks went by and I hadn't given the incident a second thought, when Charlie asked, "Where's your Scofield Bible?"

"Uh . . . remember those guys that were hitchhiking that I called you about?"

"You didn't give them your Bible, did you?"

"I had to," I replied with a big grin. "You wouldn't let me bring them home so I went to Eleanor's and got some money from her to give to them so they could get a motel room. When I went to give them some Christian literature, I realized I didn't have any with me and so I gave them my Bible."

Everything by Prayer

Charlie just shook his head, wondering what in the world he was going to do with me.

Over a year had passed and adventure after adventure had gone by. The two hitchhikers were the last thing on my mind when I went to the mailbox that summer day.

As usual, I was believing God to take care of our needs. He had never let us down since the day we started life together and I knew He would continue to get us through the hard times. I had been praying earnestly for $10. That doesn't sound like much, but when you don't have it and need it, it can sure seem like a lot.

I opened the mailbox and there was a package with a Savannah return address. What a surprise when I opened it and saw my Scofield Bible along with a beautiful *thank you* card and a $10 bill!

The two young men had not forgotten the promise they made to me that night to return my Bible. I had totally forgotten that promise and since I had other bibles, I didn't miss the one I had given away. I still had the God of the Bible in my heart, which is more important than any words printed on paper.

I must admit, it was with great fanfare and a little bit of smugness, that I revealed to Charlie the contents of the day's mail!

Help me LORD, to continue to trust you, not only for the big things, but even for the little things. YOU are a faithful, prayer answering God.

Chapter 13 - GROWING IN SPECIFIC FAITH

*"But grow in grace, and in the knowledge of our Lord and Savior Jesus Christ.
To him be glory both now and forever. Amen."
2 Peter 3:18*

Figure 36 - INDIAN ORPHAN WITH JERRI - 1997

Her name was Daisy Gibson and she was my neighbor in California. Daisy was the sweetest, kindest and craziest woman I had ever met. Daisy prayed about everything, including her fried eggs.

Since I had only been a Christian for five years (this was the early '60s), I looked up to Daisy as a teacher and mentor. She was a bit older than me in the natural and much older than me in the spiritual.

When Daisy told me that she prayed every time she cracked an egg that the yolk wouldn't break, I thought that was a little crazy, until I tried it and it worked!

I began by asking God for little things and by 2019 I have grown enough to pray specifically and believe God for really big things; answers that apart from faith would never have happened.

My Christian life matured and my faith grew stronger. The day came in 1974 when we started our 2,500-mile journey across the United States during the oil embargo gas shortage to find the country home of our dreams. We had been quite specific when we prayed about the size of the acreage and the age of the house we wanted. We felt quite satisfied when the realtor told us the old farmhouse (1885) was on 7 acres. We figured that God, in His wisdom, had split the difference with us in our request for a house on 5-10 acres.

Two of the *specific* things we had asked God for was a piano and a good working fireplace. Note: I said piano and good working fireplace. We should have added, *good working* to our piano request also.

What a delight when we were given the keys to the house and saw that the former owners had left their piano. I rushed to the upright piano and opened it to see beautiful ivory keys. I sat down and hit a few keys and to my surprise there was no sound.

We opened the cover at the top of the piano and were shocked to see that nothing was inside. Nothing! I was crushed. Charlie laughed and said, "Maybe we weren't specific enough honey."

Soon Charlie had the empty piano loaded and on the way to the dump. I guess it was so light that the wind caught it and it fell off the truck. So much for a piano, but I need to add that the fireplace was so good it would suck the socks right off your feet if you were sitting in front of it!

Fast forward to the '90s and my faith was growing by leaps and bounds. We had seen so many answers to specific prayers that we had to hold onto our hats because we never knew where the next adventure would be happening.

While attending a Full Gospel Businessmen's Association meeting we heard a young Indian couple share a short testimony. I immediately thought that I needed to ask the couple to come to Cochran for lunch. I had an ulterior motive. I knew a Cochran resident who was from India and I was hoping the couple might be able to share Jesus with him.

After lunch, our friend went back to work, and Edith the young Indian woman, said, "You need to meet my mom. She lives in India and has a Bible school and an orphanage."

I smiled sweetly and thought, "Thanks, but no thanks!" I had never had the first desire to go to India. I thought that was the end of it, but I was wrong.

Laughingly, I had shared the incident with a few friends and even some family members. One day I went to the mailbox and there was a card with a $500 check and a note that said, "This is to sow into your upcoming trip to India."

What?

Shortly thereafter our daughter sold her pet store and she handed me a check for $350. "What's this for?" I asked.

"This is for the orphans in India, Mom."

By this time, it seemed that perhaps God was planning something bigger than me here. Charlie said, "Maybe we need to pray about this, honey. It sounds to me like God might want you to go to India."

A few weeks later we were at the Holiday Inn in Cordele, GA where we were counselors at a marriage seminar. We were seated for dinner at a large banquet table for eight. The only person I knew was a lady across from me. I spoke to her about my upcoming trip to India. By this time enough money

Everything by Prayer

had come in for me to purchase a round trip ticket but there was a slight glitch: I would have an 18-hour layover in Kuala Lumpur, the capital of Malaysia.

I told her about the layover and the man seated next to me asked me what city I would be in for the 18-hour layover. I told him I couldn't pronounce it, but that it was the capital.

The man quickly peeled off the name and told me he had been a missionary there for 20 years and not to worry about a thing because he would handle everything for me.

The ball was rolling.

In preparation for the trip, I had been fasting three days a week. During this time, I wrote pages and pages in my journal of things the Lord was sharing with me. One day the Holy Spirit spoke to me: "I want you to give $1,000 to Padma (Edith's mother) for the orphanage."

I was jubilant. I immediately shared the message from God with Charlie, and he said, "Where are you going to get that kind of money?"

"I don't know," I answered, "but I have no doubt it's coming!" Already money had poured in for my trip. I had not asked for one red cent, but my ticket had been paid and my new missionary friend had already arranged meetings for me in Malaysia.

A week later at a meeting for Women's Aglow in Norman Park, GA a friend walked up to me and handed me a check for $1,000. When I gushed, "Oh, I can't wait to tell you where this money is going. . . . ." She shook her head and said, "I don't want to hear it. I didn't want to give it to you. I told the Lord you already had your ticket. He told me to give it to you anyway because 'You, have no idea what she is praying to me about!'"

A few weeks later I arrived in Malaysia. The airline had arranged a ride to a beautiful hotel. The next morning a chauffeur driven Mercedes pulled up to the hotel and I was ushered into the car for a drive to a high-rise office building.

Figure 37 - KUALA LUMPUR - MALASIA

On the 40th floor about fifty people were gathered in a large room, waiting to hear me share my testimony and the good news about Jesus. From there we went to a private home where a luncheon had been prepared with thirty women in attendance. The hostess for this event was the wife of the head of the Full Gospel Businessmen's Association in all of Asia!

From there I was whisked off to the airport where I boarded a flight to continue my journey to India. While in India so many wonderful things happened, things I will share in another chapter; but suffice it to say, learning to pray specifically has benefits that are out of this world!

Chapter 14 - THE RAINS WILL COME TOMORROW

"For verily I say unto you, That whosoever shall say unto this mountain, Be thou removed, and be thou cast into the sea; and shall not doubt in his heart, but shall believe that those things which he saith shall come to pass; he shall have whatsoever he saith."
Mark 11:23

Figure 38 - JERRI PREACHING AT CRUSADE IN INDIA

Arriving in India in August of 1997 was quite the experience. The Lord had provided all the funds; from my ticket to the extra $1,000 for Padma Mudalier's orphanage in Madras.

My adventures in Malaysia were still whirling around in my head as the plane was landing. It was hard to believe I was finally halfway around the world in the very country where Thomas the Apostle had gone to share the Gospel 2,000 years ago.

As I got off the airplane I was surrounded by a population of mostly short and dark-skinned Indians. You might say that *I stuck out like a sore thumb*. There was no way to hide my fair skin, blonde hair and 5'8" stature.

Shouts of "Taxi! Taxi!" filled the air as eager taxicab drivers were vying for my attention and my business. As I looked over the sea of humanity, I felt a little panicky until I saw this beautiful woman wearing a white sari coming toward me with a big smile and outstretched arms.

"Miss Jerri. It's really you! Welcome to India!"

I breathed a sigh of relief, gave her a big hug and off we went to the local YWCA where I would be spending a portion of my time while in India for the next three weeks.

I might add here that I really had no idea what I was doing in India, other than coming to bless the children in Padma's orphanage. I had one huge suitcase filled with goodies for the orphans. It was loaded with Tootsie Pops, tee-shirts with pictures of children from various areas of the world with a message of Jesus' love and special, green-colored sunglasses.

Prior to flying to India, I had received a letter from Padma requesting my picture. I had no idea what she was planning to do with it. I was in for the surprise of my life! Padma, as it turned out, was head of a large group of pastors in Southern India and she had told everyone that a very famous woman evangelist from America was coming to preach. Who? Me?

There were flyers everywhere with my smiling face and an invitation to come hear me preach. Posters were on buildings and in one city a big banner stretched across a street with my picture plastered on it. Talk about surprised.

First stop after dropping off one of my suitcases at the YWCA was the orphanage. There is no way to describe how much fun it was to present the candy, tee-shirts and sunglasses to all the children. There were great squeals of delights and a lot of picture taking.

After a short lunch Padma took me back to my room and told me to be ready to preach that evening and she would be my interpreter. I closed my door and dropped to my knees at my bedside and cried, "Lord. I have no idea what I'm going to say. I didn't come to preach, but you saw all the posters . . . help!"

As I prayed, with tears streaming down my face, I heard the Lord speaking to my heart. "You have been praying and fasting for three months. You have been writing down in your journal messages from My word. Those messages were not just for you . . . they were for India."

Figure 39 - TEE SHIRTS & SUNGLASSES FOR INDIAN ORPHANS - 1997

I began to breathe again and dug into my suitcase to pull out my journal. Sure enough, the things I had written began to make sense. I could see the Lord's hand on what I had written. Page after page bore insights from Him for the hungry hearts in India.

I called home and told Charlie what had happened, and his quiet, calm assurance brought additional peace to my heart. God was right there with me in India. He would help me.

Since my visit was during Monsoon season all the meetings were scheduled at inside venues. The adventure was about to start. In addition to Charlie's prayers were the prayers of students in my 6th grade Sunday school class. I had asked the kids to pray that it wouldn't rain while I was in India. During Monsoon season ministry can be a big problem because of the heavy rains. Greg Fetz, one of my students, stormed Heaven with his prayers for dry weather. Each time I called during that three-week period Charlie would say, "Greg's still praying!"

During my three weeks in India, I preached 34 times! I spoke in churches, schools, nursing homes, auditoriums and prisons. At one meeting there were approximately 5,000 people in attendance. When I returned to my room after preaching to that huge crowd; I was humbled as never before.

Shortly after I got saved in 1957, I saw myself preaching before thousands. I had never shared that with anyone, but just put it on the back burner of my mind. As I sat pondering that meeting with that huge crowd, I realized it had taken 40 years for that vision to come to pass, but it happened just as I had seen it in my vision.

Before my trip, I had familiarized myself with Hinduism, the dominant religion in India. In Hinduism many gods are worshipped. I knew there was demonic activity there and hence my burden to fast and pray. At one meeting Padma and I were on stage in a theater. I was getting ready to speak when we heard a loud scream, as a man fell from the rafters.

I have no idea what the man was doing up there, but I just knew he was up to no good. He fell at my feet and looked dead. Padma pointed her finger at him and shouted, "In the mighty Name of Jesus get up and get out of here!" The man immediately jumped up and ran out of the building.

Prayers were offered for individuals after the meetings and many sick and infirmed persons came up for prayer. Although I had constant contact with those who were ill, there was absolutely no effect on me. One pastor told me I was the first person that had ever come to visit with him at his church who had never gotten sick on their mission trip to India!

The Rains Will Come Tomorrow

Figure 40 - TYPICAL MONSOON RAINS IN INDIA

The last day I was there I ministered in three different venues. At my very last meeting a man asked me to pray that it would rain. He told me they were really in need of rain in the area. I told him that it was my fault; and that it would rain the next day. He smiled and bowed (as is their custom) and we both went our separate ways.

The next day, my time in India had come to an end. I got into the taxi that was to take me to the airport and the rains started to fall. By the time I got onto the airplane it was raining very hard. Soon our airplane was flying high above the clouds and I was on my way back to Georgia.

Only eternity will reveal the results of that mission trip. Who would believe a burden for an Indian man in Cochran, would lead to me inviting an Indian couple for lunch, that would then lead to an invitation to go to India? I do, it happened to me.

Chapter 15 - GOD AND THE WEATHER

"And they feared exceedingly, and said to one another, 'Who can this be, that even the wind and the sea obey Him!'"
Mark 4:41

Figure 41 - Ominous Clouds Over Bleckley County Courthouse

When you quit learning, you quit living. My entire life in Christ has been one of learning. Not only learning truths in the Bible but learning how those truths can be incorporated into everyday life!

It's great to read how Jesus spoke to the wind and the waves, but what about us in our daily lives? Can we really speak to the elements and see them move and change? I believe so!

I had been a Christian many years before I experienced this in my own life. I had read about the miracles that Jesus performed, commanding the wind to stop, but it's another thing to live in Georgia where winds can become tornados, and tornados can bring death and destruction.

Learning about the power of confession was eye opening to me. When I discovered that our tongue has the power of life and death (Proverbs 18:21), I began to pay closer attention to what I was saying. Jesus had talked about this to His disciples one day on the road to Jerusalem as recorded in Mark 11.

In that portion of Scripture we read where He cursed a fig tree and then He followed up the example of the fig tree's demise with these words, "For whosoever shall SAY unto this mountain, 'be thou removed' and not doubt in his heart, he shall have whatsoever he SAYS." Wow!

Figure 42 – TORNADO COMING OUR WAY

Little by little I began to incorporate positive confession, with biblical directives into my vocabulary. I was seeing more and more answers to prayer by doing so.

During this period in the early eighties our two youngest girls were in college and had signed up for a program with Coca-Cola. The soft drink company had issued a grant to help students in high school; students who came from low income families. They wanted these students to learn about social graces by frequenting high class restaurants and various activities costing high dollars.

Our girls became mentors and had a great time living the high life taking these kids on tours, eating in various fancy restaurants and generally just having fun with them, all the while getting paid for doing so. Tough assignment!

As a result of spending a great deal of time with these kids every week they became more than mentors . . . they became friends. Several of the kids began to attend a weekly Bible study we held in our home for college young people.

One evening we had a guest speaker coming who had lived a homosexual lifestyle, but who had become convinced through his study of Scriptures that this was not the life God intended for him to live.

Since two of the high school students were involved in this lifestyle, we were very excited about the evening and were praying for the Holy Spirit to do a mighty work that night.

About an hour before the kids were to arrive the sky started to darken. As it got darker and darker in the living room, I decided to go out onto the front porch to get a better look. Across the highway a tornado was approaching. I screamed for Dotty to come outside. Within seconds she came out and she was as horrified as I was.

I said, "Hold up your hand!" We both held up our right arms toward the approaching tornado and I yelled, "In the Name of Jesus, TORNADO TURN!!"

Instantly the tornado turned left and we both began to yell praises to our awesome God for what we had just witnessed. As a result of this miracle we had a great Bible study that night and both of those young men turned their lives over to Jesus!

Fast forward to 2004 and we were about to have our first Bible Reading Marathon in our town and in our state!

Everything was lined up perfectly for our opening, but apparently the forces of darkness were not happy about the Word of God being proclaimed from the steps of our courthouse.

Figure 43 – PINE TREE DANGEROUSLY CLOSE TO THE HOUSE

I had gone to Cochran City Hall to talk with the mayor and as I was about to leave the building the Chief of Police came up to me and said, "Jerri, you're not going to be able to have that marathon tonight. Look outside. It's going to rain."

Without hesitation I said, "It will NOT rain — in the Name of Jesus!" He just shook his head in disbelief. I'm sure he was thinking I was crazy, but not only did it NOT rain, it has never rained during our opening ceremony in all 16 years of our history of holding Bible Reading Marathons!

As we approached the opening night of our 16th Annual Bible Reading Marathon all the weather reports were broadcasting 100% chance of rain. Again, I stood on God's promises to bless our opening night and declared in the name of Jesus that it would not rain!

I believe everyone was astounded as our opening night was one of the best in all sixteen years without a single cloud in the sky. So much for weather reports.

God and the Weather

Charlie too, has experienced the power that the name of Jesus holds against the elements. While helping some friends by cutting down pine trees in their yard, his saw got stuck in the tree. The tree had a malformation called a dog leg in it; causing the tree to lean and settle on his saw. There was nothing he could do. The tree was leaning toward the roof of the house and a catastrophe was in the making.

Our son Jeff was with him and Charlie told him to go to the hardware store and get a rope so they could pull the tree away from the house. Jeff promptly got in the truck and headed to the hardware store.

While Jeff was gone a powerful wind came up and wouldn't you know it . . . the wind was blowing toward the house and disaster was about to happen.

Charlie held his hand up and yelled, "Wind, in the NAME OF JESUS, I command you to stop!"

We learned later, that at the very same time this was happening, the couple who owned the house were vacationing many miles away at Callaway Gardens, when an interesting conversation occurred.

As they were leisurely walking around a lake, homeowner Raymond Smoot said to his wife, "Do you really think Charlie is as good at cutting down pine trees as Jerri says he is?"

Carolyn answered, "Of course he is!"

Raymond said, "I think we need to pray for him, Carolyn." They stopped in their tracks and prayed that God would help Charlie as he cut the pine trees down for them.

When Jeff finally returned with the rope (the brakes on the truck had gone out), he saw his daddy standing there beside the tree in awe. The wind had stopped blowing and all Charlie could say was, "Let's get this done!"

Everything by Prayer

They attached the rope to the tree and then to the pickup truck, pulling the tree in the opposite direction away from the house. Just another day in the life and adventures of Charlie and Jerri Tuck.

When I returned home from work that evening, I saw Charlie sitting in his chair in the living room. I asked how everything had gone at Raymond and Carolyn's house. He just shook his head and said, "I'd rather not talk about it right now."

From that day on I never volunteered Charlie's tree cutting services, but we both learned from personal experience that when the situation warrants it, we can count on God to control the weather!

Chapter 16 - WHETHER A MOLE HILL OR A MOUNTAIN

"Now to Him who is able to do exceedingly abundantly above all that we ask or think, according to the power that works in us."
Ephesians 3:20

Figure 44 - WHETHER A MOLE HILL OR A MOUNTAIN

Growing in faith is most definitely a process. As I look back over 62+ years of walking with the Lord and trusting Him for everything from Easter baskets to real estate purchases, I can truly say that God does over and above, *everything we could ask or think.*

In studying about the faith of Moses' mother I think there is a very valuable lesson for all of us. Yes, Jochebed had faith that God would take care of her baby, but at the same time she had a part in that answer. With loving hands, she wove a basket in which to place her three-month-old baby boy.

As we pray and put our faith in our Heavenly Father, there are times . . . many times, that we must *do something*.

I remember when that *something* was a search for the perfect Christmas tree. Charlie took our five little Tucks out into the woods that surrounded our old farmhouse.

At this period in our lives we couldn't afford to purchase a Christmas tree and so the logical thing to do was to find one, cut it down and bring it home. Sound easy? Not exactly.

Our first Christmas, although meager monetarily, proved to be a memorable one for the children. As they optimistically tramped through the woods, just knowing they would find a beautiful Christmas tree, they began to grow weary after nearly an hour of searching.

The little ones were beginning to get tired and restless in the search and the older ones were growing discouraged. Every tree under consideration seemed to have a flaw that disqualified it. Either it was too small or too tall, too bushy or not bushy enough, too crooked or just too plain ugly! What to do?

Finally, Charlie stopped and said, "Look kids. We need to pray and ask the Lord to show us where the perfect tree is." They joined hands in a circle and Charlie prayed. He ended the prayer with the usual *Amen!* Then, the sound of a tinkling bell was heard.

Startled, Charlie asked, "Did you kids hear that bell?" They all said yes and excitedly they started going toward the sound of the bell. Deeper and deeper they went into the woods, until the sound of the bell ceased and there, right in front of them, was the most beautiful tree they had ever seen! After cutting it down they triumphantly marched home to show their mother and give the exciting details of how they found the perfect tree!

The following Spring the children had planted their very own garden, but a problem occurred, and we all seemed at a loss, including the top farmer, Charlie Tuck! The plants kept mysteriously showing up, laying on top of the ground, not entirely eaten, but obviously something under the ground was eating the roots and then the plants just flopped over.

Remembering the great answer to prayer about the beautiful Christmas tree, Charlie asked the kids to join him in prayer about the mystery of the dead plants laying upon the ground.

There was no hesitation as the children joined hands around the little garden. Their faith was growing. They couldn't wait to see what would happen when their daddy said *Amen!* Nope! No tinkling bells and no obvious answer. Charlie told them that sometimes we don't get answers immediately, but just know that God had heard their prayers.

The next day they ran expectantly out to the garden and there was the answer in plain sight! A mole was lying dead upon the ground next to a lifeless plant. Apparently, God had sent a bird who *just happened* to be flying nearby when the culprit mole had surfaced after eating the roots on the plant and attacked him.

The result was two-fold: the little garden flourished and the faith of five little Tucks grew stronger again. To be perfectly honest, not only was their faith growing, but so was ours.

Needing more income, I called our local newspaper to put in an ad for babysitting. While talking with Jewel NeSmith the editor, we got into a conversation about how the Tucks arrived in Cochran all the way from California.

After about 15 minutes of talking and laughing about the whole travel episode, Ms. NeSmith asked me if I would write the story of our trip as an article for the paper.

I protested, saying I didn't know how to write anything. She encouraged me and said to write it just like I had told it to her in our phone conversation.

Seated in front of my old Royal typewriter I began to pound out the story. The more I typed the easier the words flowed. I called it, *The Journey*. I took the typed story to her office and left it with her secretary, thinking that was the end of the matter.

About a week later I was mopping my kitchen floor when I heard the Lord speaking to my spirit and He said, "Ms. NeSmith is going to get so many responses about your story that she is going to ask you to write a weekly column." I just laughed and kept on mopping.

Strange as it may seem, as I mopped the floor, one idea after another popped into my mind and with my Royal typewriter nearby, I would stop and type the idea and then resume mopping. Within 40 minutes I had pounded out 45 ideas for articles.

A few days later Ms. NeSmith called and said, almost verbatim, the very words the Lord had spoken to my heart. Not only was I going to write a weekly article, she was going to pay me $5 for each article. As a side note . . . no one ever called to answer my ad for babysitting. Whew!

About a year after I started writing my weekly column, *Just Jerri*, Ms. NeSmith asked me to come to work for the Cochran Journal selling advertising. My income was rising.

For several years I pounded the pavement selling ads for the paper, all the while writing my little weekly column. The Lord was providing through my little efforts, along with Charlie's sale of goats and rabbits, and of course with his paycheck as a civil servant at Robins Air Force Base.

One day a friend of mine asked me if I would like to meet the State News Editor for the Macon Telegraph and News. I had heard of Bill Boyd and I was excited to get an opportunity to meet him.

Over lunch Bill told me he was looking for a feature writer for the Cochran-Bleckley area for his newspaper. I have no idea where my confidant answer came from, but I smiled and said, "You're looking at her!"

Figure 45 - WAS IT THE TINKER BELL FAIRY?

He looked at me with a smile and challenged, "Don't tell me. Show me!"

I then proceeded to tell him that I taught a Bible study in our home for college students and that one of the students was a blind girl and her life would make a wonderful feature story.

That initial story was my introduction to becoming, not only a feature writer for the newspaper, but also a reporter. I was eventually offered the job as Bureau Chief for the paper in Dublin, GA thirty miles away. I turned down this position because raising children was more of a priority at this time. My income was growing and so was my confidence in God as my provider.

I first married at age 15 in 1955. Things were a lot different back in those days. I was told by a high school administrator that I could no longer attend school. They considered me a *bad influence*. Like I said, times have changed!

Without a high school diploma, I felt like I was doing pretty good, however my husband felt I needed to stretch a little and get my GED. "I don't need a GED," I said, "I'm doing fine without one." I didn't mention that I didn't think I was smart enough to pass the test.

Charlie kept after me until I finally gave in and went to a neighboring county where GED tests were being offered. This was in 1977 before classes were available to learn how to pass a GED test. To say I was nervous was an understatement.

Halfway through the testing I called Charlie and in tears I said, "I can't do this. I have to take a math test and I don't know anything about math."

"Yes, you can," he said encouragingly. "You're going to pass it." Passing a math test seemed to be one of the biggest mountains I had ever ventured to tackle. In high school I had taken an aptitude test and I had scored 98% in English and 2% in Math.

Wiping the tears off my cheeks I went back into the classroom. As I looked at the questions on the test, I sent up a prayer, knowing Charlie was at home praying for me too.

Surprise! I passed the test, got my GED certificate and promptly threw it into a drawer. Little did I know that when I decided to enter the real estate profession, I would need either a high school diploma, or a GED certificate in order to take the course. God was on the move in our lives and He was providing every need according to His riches in glory by Christ Jesus! (Phil. 4:19)

Chapter 17 - WELCOME TO WVMG

"Trust in the LORD *with all thine heart; and lean not unto thine own understanding. In all thy ways acknowledge him, and he shall direct thy paths."*
Proverbs 3:5-6

Figure 46 - IN THE WVMG STUDIO - (L-R) KRISTY CRANFORD, VIRGINIA TUCK, SARAH TYSON, DOTTY TUCK & HONG VO

Working as a news reporter was not quite as fun as being a feature writer. I've always felt that everyone has a story and so it seemed easy to do that type of writing, but when it came to news . . . that was something else!

Case in point, we had a gut-wrenching kidnapping and subsequent murder in December of 1976. Two men went into a small Cochran convenience store, robbed it of $466 and kidnapped the young 18-year-old female clerk, Teresa Allen. Subsequently the men raped, then shot her, leaving her lifeless body in the bushes to rot.

Everything by Prayer

Two days after the murder, Teresa Allen's body was found near GA HWY 41 in Monroe County. I will never forget that awful day as Bill was asked to notify Teresa's parents that she had been found and was dead.

During the Viet Nam War Bill Boyd, a former Marine, had the job of notifying families of those Marines who had been killed or injured. I guess that's why he was chosen for this task, but I was not about to go with him and waited in the car.

When Bill returned to the car, I was crying my eyeballs out. "That's it," I said between sobs. "I quit! I don't care if the town is burning down, I'm through with news reporting."

Figure 47 - MY NAME IS ON THE ROLL

Bill, who was usually gruff, said, "OK Tuck. I'm going cut you some slack because you have kids, but you'll be fine!"

Instead of being fine, the situation got worse.

The hunt for Teresa's killers went into January of the following year. Finally, after weeks of agonizing false leads, they were both arrested and jailed. One of the men escaped temporarily, but eventually was captured, tried and executed.

During this entire situation, Bill Boyd (State News Editor) and I were working on the case night and day. When one of the killers escaped from the Cochran city jail, I was a nervous wreck. I just knew he was coming after me for writing all the stories about the awful crime.

After the killer's execution I decided to quit the newspaper business. I was mentally and emotionally drained by the entire ordeal and friends of mine had just purchased a local radio station and asked me to come to work for them.

With my experience in advertising sales at the Cochran Journal, I began selling ads for the radio station. John Johnson, one of the owners asked me if I would like to try my hand at becoming a disc jockey. This was certainly a challenge and one that I jumped into with gusto.

As I interacted on live radio, I not only introduced music, interviewed guests, but also read the weather reports. I can still remember my kids saying, "Mom. Stop it! All the kids know you're talking to us when you say, 'Snuffy Smith says it's going to rain today so you better get those clothes off the clothesline.'"

Eventually, I had a program called, *Saturday Morning with Miss Jerri* when I held Bible classes in various churches and interviewed children.

While being a disc jockey I was still a mom, wife and hostess for our college Bible study. It was during one of our Bible studies that a young lady was invited to come and she just *happened* to be a communications major.

Wanda came from a military family and had traveled to many places throughout the world. Her religious background was practically non-existent and so coming to a Bible study was out of her comfort zone.

The first night she attended, one of the young people gave her heart to Christ. Everyone was so excited and happy, but when I turned back toward the kitchen, I noticed Wanda standing with a skeptical look on her face.

Figure 48 - MY FEET ARE ON THE ROCK - JESUS

"Why is everyone so happy?" she questioned when she saw me looking at her.

"They're just rejoicing that Melanie got saved."

Wanda just rolled her eyes and said, "Whatever!"

Her response and attitude made me realize that Miss Wanda just might need some prayer. I began praying in earnest for her and one night decided to put some feet to my prayers and went over to the college to visit her in her dorm room.

While visiting, I told Wanda that I was a disc jockey. She was quite surprised and seemed rather thrilled when I asked her if she would like to join me sometime at the radio station to see how I made commercials.

About a week later we got together at the station and truly had a fun time. Nothing religious was discussed, but it was obvious that Wanda and I were becoming friends.

More Bible studies at our house, more prayer and then one night around midnight I got a call. "Ms. Tuck, it's me, Wanda. I just wanted you to know I got saved tonight!"

Without a doubt I knew that there was rejoicing in the presence of the angels of God. (Luke 15:10) There was also rejoicing in the Tuck household as well. I can't help but wonder if that short stint as a disc jockey, was simply God's way of getting Wanda into His fold.

Live Christian radio is something that even today, forty+ years later, I enjoy listening to. Selling radio advertising, on the other hand, is not as enjoyable as talking on the radio.

As I went from business to business, doing my best to promote WVMG and sell ads, I discovered that not everyone was enthusiastic about spending their company dollars on a little-known radio station in Middle Georgia.

One day I was sitting in a savings and loan institution in Warner Robins waiting for the advertising manager to beckon me into his office. While waiting I was thumbing through a magazine and read an article entitled, *The Ten Hardest Things to Sell*. Would you believe . . . Number One was RADIO ADVERTISING!

I began to question why I was putting myself through the difficult job of selling something you can't touch, see or feel.

The turning point came when my friends sold the radio station to a man who was going to do a 180 degree turn in broadcasting. Instead of Christian programming he was turning it into a rock and roll station.

I've always contended I believe in rock and roll . . . my feet are on THE ROCK and my name is on THE ROLL, but other than that I decided it was time to change career directions.

While on the phone with my brother in California I told him about my situation with the change in ownership of the station and he asked a question that changed my direction. "Jerri, have you ever thought of going into real estate?" That simple question catapulted me into a 28-year career from 1979-2007.

As I look back on those WVMG days I realize God was preparing me for my next step in my walk with Him. Each of us has a separate path, but those of us who belong to the family of God, know that the pathway is always leading up to Him. Nothing is ever wasted time when we allow the Lord to direct our steps.

Chapter 18 - SO, YOU WANT TO SPEAK HEBREW? OY VEY!

"For then will I turn to the people a pure language, that they may all call upon the name of the LORD, to serve him with one consent."
Zephaniah 3:9

Figure 49 - JERRI IN ISRAEL WITH IDF SOLDIERS

Someone asked me recently if I had served in the Israeli Defense Force (IDF) because they had seen a picture of me in an IDF uniform. I would have loved to answer in the affirmative, but truth be told I was just one of many volunteers with a Jewish organization called Ser-el.

Ser-el enlists people from every denomination and walk of life to volunteer for a three week 'enlistment' to do grunt work for the IDF so they can do more important things ... like fighting Hamas and Hezbollah. The only difference in our uniforms in the Ser-el organization were blue strips, sewn onto on the shoulder epaulets. I guess if a terrorist came, we could quickly point to the blue strips and say, "Wait! Don't shoot. I'm only a volunteer."

The year was 1994 when my stint in Israel took place, but a deep love for the Jewish people and land was budding in my spirit. Many years later, when an opportunity was presented to learn Hebrew, I jumped at the opportunity.

Each week, for four months, my husband and I, along with good friends, David and Nanette Whedon, traveled to Macon to learn Hebrew from Molly Smith, who was a member of a Messianic congregation, Beth Yeshua (House of Jesus).

Although none of us became fluent in speaking Hebrew, we learned the alphabet which, after all, was the sole purpose of the class. From that first baby step in learning Hebrew, an idea developed to share what we had learned with others.

My first thought was sharing this knowledge with inmates at the Bleckley County Detention Center where Charlie and I had been teaching Bible studies. At this time the center housed male inmates.

When I presented this opportunity, about 25 men expressed an interest in learning, but that's where the challenge came in. Where would I get the money (Approximately $30 per student) to buy the learning materials? Solution? Pray!

One of our sons-in-law heard about our desire to teach the class and without me asking for any money he promptly sent the needed funds. We were on our way.

When the 16-week course concluded we held a graduation. Mr. Tommy Bowen the Superintendent of the facility was floored. Some of the men had never graduated from high school, much less taken a GED course and here, during a graduation ceremony, they were speaking, singing and writing in Hebrew!

I was to learn that God's desire to see His children learn the *pure language* (Zephaniah 3:9) was quite intense. He began to stir up the idea even more in the next few years, but always it was bathed in prayer for FUNDS!

Just as I had never asked for a single dime for any of my mission trips through the years (Brazil, Ecuador, China, India, Israel, Costa Rica or Mexico) I was determined to pray in the funds. Early in my Christian life I was inspired by George Mueller who had prayed in over 9 million pounds ($11.5 million) for his orphanage in England during his lifetime.

One day a lady, whom I barely knew, called me and told me she had sold a piece of property and wanted to send me some money to help me in my prison ministry. Wow! She had no idea I was praying for funds to teach another Hebrew class.

Was I ever surprised when I found out she had donated a whopping $1,500! With this generous donation, there was not only enough money to purchase materials for the 16-week course, but also enough for me to purchase materials for an advanced course in the subject.

By the time I held the second Hebrew class the facility had changed from a detention center to a Residential Substance Abuse Training center (RSAT) for women. During the course the ladies told me of other women in the dorms who wanted to take a Hebrew class if I were to offer another one.

Laughingly, I told them they would have to pray in the money. I had told the ladies about the miraculous way funds had been provided for them to take the course and so they were encouraged and challenged to pray.

Prior to beginning this course, a very sad thing happened in our family. My brother-in-law Jim Cardoso had passed away. My sister, Kathy, asked me if I would come out to California to speak at his funeral. Without hesitation I went, counting it an amazing privilege to be asked to do so.

Jim had a very good relationship with the Lord. About five years prior to his passing I had flown out to see him and we had a wonderful time reflecting on the love of our Lord. During a private communion service in his home, Jim had fully given his heart to the Lord.

Figure 50 - JERRI WITH SISTER KATHY

Kathy offered several times to pay for my flight out there, but I was adamant in my refusal to take anything from her as I counted it such an honor and privilege to have been such a big part of something so important to her. I loved Jim and it had nothing to do with money!

Fast forward to the Hebrew class and my laughing challenge to PRAY for funds! It had been at least three or four months since Jim's passing and I called to check on my baby sister. (She and Jim were married just over 50 years and so she wasn't really a baby!)

She was doing well, but still missing Jim like crazy. During the conversation she said, "Jerri, I'm sending you $1,500." I was quick to protest, but she continued, "I'm not taking no for an answer. You can use it for your prison ministry."

Charlie and I were in the same room and I covered the phone and whispered, "I can't believe this. Those women have prayed that money in to take that Hebrew course!"

The next course saw 37 women joyfully learning Hebrew and knowing that their prayers played a big part in the provision of their Hebrew educational materials.

More time went by and dear Tommy Bowen, the Superintendent of the RSAT facility, had been transferred to a prison in Macon. He was greatly missed by all of us. He had been such a great supporter of the ministry, both when it was the Bleckley Probation Detention Center and currently as an RSAT facility.

Thankfully, by the grace of God, the ministry has been ongoing for over 16 years. Five nights a week we have faithful volunteers going inside to deliver the message of salvation through the Lord Jesus Christ.

Along with the ministry at RSAT, Charlie and I have been going into Dodge Prison in Chester, Georgia for many years delivering the Word of God to thirsty hearts. Sometimes I jokingly say, "We have a life sentence without parole." It's a funny statement, but not one bit funny to be on the wrong side of the razor wire.

In June of 2019 Charlie and I were leaving the facility when we saw Tommy Bowen walking toward us from the direction of the prison offices. We were all heading toward the front door at the same time. I was shocked when I saw him and blurted out, "What are you doing here?"

With a big grin he said, "I'm the new warden. I'll be starting next month. Are you going to teach a Hebrew class?" Charlie and I got a big laugh out of that and just put the suggestion on the back burner.

Figure 51 PATCHWORK FAMILY - 25 COPIES PLEASE

    A few months later we were met at the front gate of the prison by Chaplain Sterling Averett. The first words out of his mouth were, "Tommy Bowen says you're going to teach a Hebrew class. Is that right?"

We looked at each other and then back at the chaplain and I said, "If you want us to do one, we'll be glad to."

Back to prayer!

This time the answer came in the most unusual way (which they all seem to). Charlie had a short stint with pneumonia and while in the emergency room we met a very nice young doctor. While waiting for a room to be readied we learned the doctor was a Christian. We swapped phone numbers and later I sent him a text thanking him for his excellent care and let him know that Charlie was back at home and doing fine.

For some reason (a God reason, no doubt) I had taken a book with me to the hospital. The book was, *Patchwork Family*, which I had written several years prior. The doctor seemed intrigued with the title and so I gave it to him.

The doctor, who doesn't live in our area, sent a text a few months later asking about ordering 25 of the *Patchwork Family* books. He wanted to take them to all the emergency rooms throughout Georgia where he works and have them available for patients to read while they were waiting for treatment.

The doctor never asked me for a price, just for my address. What a shock I got when I opened the envelope and saw the check for $1,000. What???

When we got together a few weeks later, over dinner which he insisted on paying for, he said, "Use the leftover money for ministry!"

We DO have a prayer answering God! Not only did we receive enough funds for the next Hebrew class, which starts the first week in January 2020, but the good doctor also agreed to be one of the assigned prayer partners for one of the inmates who will be taking the course.

Chapter 19 - IT PAYS TO ADVERTISE

"And the Lord said to me, 'Write my answer on a billboard, large and clear, so that anyone can read it at a glance and rush to tell the others.'"
Habakkuk 2:2 (TLB)

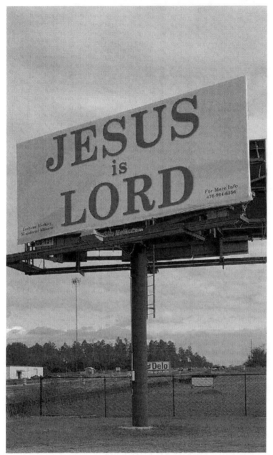

Figure 52 - "JESUS IS LORD" SIGN NORTH OF COCHRAN, GA

I think my brief career in selling newspaper and radio ads was a precursor of things to come.

One day I was at a traffic light in front of our county courthouse waiting for the light to change before proceeding, I glanced at a building located on the NW corner of our main street and for the first time really noticed the advertising displayed there.

The Dairy Queen, a pest control company and of course the gun shop, which was housed in the building, were all advertised. I kept waiting for the light to turn, all the while the wheels were turning in my head. "There should be a *Jesus is Lord* sign on that building," I mused.

Waking me out of my thoughts the light turned green and I made a quick decision. "I'm going to ask Mr. Harris if I can put a sign up," I thought. I quickly drove around the block and parked in front of his store.

"Hi Mr. Harris," I said cheerfully. "Hope you're doing well today. I was just wondering if you would mind if I put up a sign saying, 'Jesus is Lord' on the side your building?"

Mr. Harris informed me that he wouldn't have any problem with that, but he had nothing to do with the side of the building. Mr. Harris was apparently a pretty smart businessman and he had rented the side of his building to a man in Eastman, who in turn sold ads which were displayed for all to see. Pretty slick.

I quickly called the gentleman in charge of the ad space and he seemed quite receptive to my idea and said when he had time he would come up to Cochran and get together with me about the sign. Three months went by and nothing materialized.

In the meantime, not deterred in the least, I noticed another ad space in Cochran that was not filled. It was a large billboard and simply had a number plastered on the billboard, which was obviously the phone number for the billboard company.

Every week when I passed the billboard everything looked the same. Only a phone number advertised. "Hmm, *Jesus is Lord* would look really cool on that billboard." I thought.

It Pays To Advertise

Nothing had come of the ad for the building in town, so I began to think a little bigger. One day I called the number and a very nice gentleman answered and told me he would be more than happy to put JESUS IS LORD on the billboard, that is . . . until I told him I wanted it for free!

"What," he exclaimed. "Why do you think you should have it for free?"

I answered calmly, "Because it will say *JESUS IS LORD*."

Chip Pate, the salesman, told me absolutely no. The billboard was $200 a month and that was that!

Another month went by. Same question. Same answer.

After two months I asked him for his address so I could send him my book, *Gone Fishin'*. He needed to know what he was dealing with. I knew in my heart we were supposed to have that billboard declaring *JESUS IS LORD*. I kept praying. He kept saying, NO!

Finally, he wouldn't answer my calls, but I left very sweet messages on his voice mail.

In the meantime, I was going about my usual round of activities including checking my Facebook. Aha! Someone tagged me in a message they had received from Dahl McDermitt who was wondering where he could find a Christian flag. (I had received a bit of a reputation in our town about Christian flags – I'll hit that in the next chapter!)

Mr. McDermitt was not only a preacher and founder of the wonderful Refuge House (for women recovering from addictions) he was also the man in charge of the ads on Mr. Harris' building.

I quickly responded on FB and told Mr. McDermitt that he could have a Christian flag at no charge! That got his attention and a conversation by phone quickly ensued in which he told me I could put a sign up and he would let me have it for FREE! (I think I got the better deal on that one!)

To top it off Johnny Norris, at the local sign company, made the sign and had it installed and wouldn't charge me a dime. God must like ads!

Figure 53 - "JESUS IS LORD" SIGN SOUTH OF COCHRAN (L-R) JUNE SMITH, CAROLYN WILLIAMS, & EMILY DENNIS

I was ecstatic about the sign going up on the very same day we had a meeting for the Cochran-Bleckley Ministerial Alliance, of which I'm privileged to be the secretary. I told the group the story about the sign on our main street and they were all very happy with the announcement. Then I proceeded to tell them, "That's not the best news. We're going to have a billboard on Hwy 23 that says, *JESUS IS LORD.*"

It Pays To Advertise

Admittedly a few of the pastors looked a bit skeptical, especially when I told them it was going to be for free. I was partly right as you will see.

Month after month continued to go by and it was well into a year of my calling Mr. Pate when I finally got through to a secretary. She told me she would be glad to connect me to his voice mail.

As sweetly as I could answer I said, "I've left message after message on his voice mail, but he never returns my calls."

Shortly after that call, Mr. Pate called. "Ok, Jerri. You're going to get your billboard."

"Am I getting it for free?" I asked.

"No, but you can have it for $53 a month."

"Well, if that's the best you can do," I paused . . . "I guess I'll have to go with that," I responded.

I was dancing around the house when I hung up the phone. I was excited, to say the least. If I had to pay $53 a month for a billboard I would do it. I began sending texts to the preachers and telling them I had some exciting news and to call me when they had some free time.

My phone started ringing off the hook and preacher after preacher offered to help with the fees for the billboard. Before the evening was over the entire years rent was paid and then came a phone call at 11:15 pm. It was Chip Pate.

"Miss Jerri," he began. "I just felt like I needed to call you and tell you what is going on in my life." That was a phone call lasting 58 minutes and one that had me absolutely floored.

In the course of conversation Chip told me personal details of his life, which had been going downhill a long time. Between sobs he told me he could have rented the billboard out many times, but each time he went to do it he heard the Lord tell him, "That's MY billboard!!"

Everything by Prayer

Wow! So, God is more interested in people than billboards? Right!

That was the start of many months of talking to him and his wife by phone and texts of encouragement and prayers going back and forth. Today I'm glad to report their marriage is stronger than ever and they are both actively serving the Lord together in their church!

In the meantime, I shared Chip's story with a friend and asked him and his wife to pray for them. Not only did my friends pray, they told me they owned some property on the south end of town on Hwy 23 and had rented a small portion to a billboard company.

Apparently, the billboard company had been unable to rent the space, but wanted to continue the lease, amounting to $800 a year. My friends told me to contact the owners of the billboard and let them know if they would let me put up *JESUS IS LORD* on their sign, they wouldn't charge them any rent for a year. Wow!

As I drove off that day the Holy Spirit reminded me... "You asked me if there was another billboard on the opposite end of town to show you where it was. This is it!"

Glory to God! We now have two huge billboards in Cochran declaring *JESUS IS LORD*. And when both billboards were declaring this life saving announcement, I discovered this was the declaration of the early church. Instead of saying, "Nero is Lord" the Christians would answer, *"JESUS IS LORD"*

Chapter 20 - IS THERE A CHRISTIAN FLAG?

"We will rejoice in thy salvation, and in the name of our God we will set up our banners: the LORD fulfil all thy petitions."
Psalm 20:5

Figure 54 - CHRISTIAN FLAG ON BLECKLEY COUNTY COURTHOUSE

Starting up an Annual Bible Reading Marathon was a big step, but I was to learn that it wasn't the last step in the journey of public pronouncements.

I vividly remember the morning in 2005 when we were preparing to hold our 2nd Bible Reading Marathon. It was Friday and the spring air was crisp and the sky overhead was crystal clear blue. Sitting next to me on a bench in front of the courthouse was Mike Polsky, the Bleckley County Commissioner.

"Hey Jerri," he asked, "Is there such a thing as a Christian flag?"

I answered, "Yes" and wondered where this conversation was going.

Motioning to one of the pillars at the front of the courthouse he said, "What do you think would happen if I put one up there."

"Well," realizing he meant any possible pushback to having a flag hoisted with a Christian symbol on it, I answered, "I would just do it first and apologize later." End of conversation.

Later that afternoon Mike had procured a Christian flag and had the courthouse custodian install it on the pillar. Boy, were people going to be in for a big surprise when they gathered that evening for the opening ceremony. I tried to block negative thoughts out of my mind and just prayed there would be no trouble from him taking this bold step.

Just before the opening ceremony I saw Richard Harris, President of the local NAACP, staring at the prominently displayed Christian flag. Grabbing the bull by the horn while pointing at the flag, I said, "Richard, isn't that amazing? Wow! A Christian flag hanging from our courthouse! We are truly blessed!"

Richard didn't say anything right then, but when the opening ceremony was over a bunch of us, including our special opening night speaker, State Senator Ross Tolleson, headed to a local restaurant. Richard and his wife Doris also went with us.

As we entered the restaurant Richard whispered to me, "I want to talk with you privately after dinner." Inwardly, I was nervous as I was certain it was about the display of the Christian flag at the courthouse.

Blocking out a possible confrontation about the flag I was determined to enjoy the moment with Senator Tolleson and others who had a part in the opening of our second BRM.

Is There A Christian Flag?

Figure 55 - CITY HALL FLAG RAISING - 2012

As we ate and conversed over a delicious dinner, we were all rejoicing over the great crowd who attended the opening ceremony and so grateful we were able to hold this public event to honor God and His word.

Leaving the restaurant there were the usual hugs and goodbyes, but I noticed Richard hanging back. "Okay," I thought. "This is it. He's going to lambast me good about that flag."

"You wanted to talk with me, Richard?" I asked.

"Yes," he said with a serious tone. "Jerri, I am so impressed with all that went on this evening and I just wanted you to know that I think you would make a great president for our Cochran-Bleckley Chamber of Commerce."

Well, that was certainly unexpected. I just laughed and said, "Why, thank you Richard. That is so sweet of you, but I don't feel like I'm the right person for that job. Thank you for thinking of me."

Whew!

For the next few years Mr. Polsky would put the Christian flag up during our annual marathons and then in 2009, at the conclusion of the event, the custodian was putting the podium, chairs and other event trappings away. I was watching him and while up on a ladder, by the pillar displaying the Christian flag, he yelled down at me, "What do you want me to do with this?"

"Just leave it," I said.

From that point the flag was flying 24/7. Each time the flag got a bit frayed, Mr. Polsky would purchase a new one. I was thrilled beyond words.

In 2012 I received a call from one of the members of the Cochran City Council, Dell Daniels. Ms. Daniels wanted me to know what a blessing one of my recent columns (Just Jerri) had meant to her. She let me know that she read them every week, but this week's article had truly ministered to her.

I had never met Ms. Daniels, but when we finished discussing my piece in the Cochran Journal, I asked her if she had noticed the Christian flag flying from the courthouse.

When she told me that she had noticed, I then pushed the needle and said, "Wouldn't it be great if we had one flying from Cochran City Hall?"

Her answer? "Consider it done!"

Dell went right out, purchased a Christian flag and the next thing I knew I was being invited to a flag raising at the city hall. Acting Mayor, Willie Basby, had his staff, council members and other city employees out in the front of the building when I arrived.

Each person was given a piece of paper with the Pledge of Allegiance to the Christian Flag written out. What a day that was! We even got a great picture of us all holding the Christian flag before it was hoisted on the flagpole. With great solemnity

Is There A Christian Flag?

we held our hands over our hearts and repeated the pledge together.

Figure 56 - CHRISTIAN FLAG OVER COCHRAN CITY HALL

I pledge allegiance to the Christian flag and to the Savior for whose kingdom it stands. One Savior, crucified, buried and risen again, with life and liberty to all who believe.

Everything by Prayer

As I drove off that day, I was in total amazement of what God had just done. Driving down E. Dykes Street toward home I noticed for the first time that the Mathis Funeral Home had a flagpole.

I grabbed my cell phone and called Danny Mathis (back in the day it was legal to talk on a cell phone while driving). "Hey, Danny, guess what just happened!"

After I told Danny about the flag raising event he responded with, "Absolutely. We'll get one and get it right up."

"Well, that was easy," I thought. Continuing my drive toward home I thought about another funeral home on the other end of town, but on the same street. "I wouldn't want to leave Fisher Funeral Home out," I thought, "I better call Joe."

Not only did Fisher Funeral Home and Mathis Funeral home get on board, but so did the Cochran-Bleckley Chamber of Commerce, Georgia Farm Bureau, New Life Church of God, Cannon Auto Sales, Welcome Friends, A & H Storage, Alco Insurance, Bleckley County Courthouse, Cochran City Hall and Promise of Hope.

When I counted them up, I was delighted to see there were 12 altogether. Private businesses, county and city governmental businesses, a church and a rehab facility. Some of these venues began to fly the flag all year long, not just during the Bible Reading Marathon. Praise God!

During the next few years the idea of flying a Christian flag caught on in the community. One year I distributed over 1,000 flags. 110 businesses in our town were flying the Christian flag. One business owner told me that he thought it was the new Georgia flag! We even had two Hindu businesses and one Buddhist run business flying the Christian flag. Cochran was making a statement!

In 2013 we were honored to have a member of the American Center for Law and Justice (ACLJ) staff as our keynote speaker for the BRM. Andrew Ekonomou was also the Assistant

Is There A Christian Flag?

District Attorney in Brunswick, Georgia. He was so impressed with all the Christian flags everywhere he couldn't contain his enthusiasm.

As he stood before the crowd of several hundred persons in the audience he said, in a serious and firm tone, "If anyone ever tries to stop this Bible Reading Marathon, you just call me!"

The devil had had enough. Gathering his crew together he began to fight the Christian flags flying at the city hall and the courthouse. Then, with the help of the Freedom From Religion Foundation (FFRF) he aimed at the actual Bible Reading Marathon event.

Hmm. Mr. Ekonomou said to call him. I did!

The result was a four-page letter from Jay Sekulow, President and Founder of the ACLJ. The letter was sent to our county commissioner and our county attorney. The letter stated, with total clarity, that we had a legal right to hold a Bible Reading Marathon at our courthouse.

During the fight over the Christian flag flying I prayed to God and said, "Lord, why do they hate the Christian flag so much?"

He whispered to my heart that night, "Because the cross on the flag is empty . . . Satan knows he's defeated."

I went peacefully to sleep.

The next day a couple came to my front door to pick up a flag they had ordered. When I opened the door, I saw a couple of boxes. Knowing they contained flags I asked the gentleman if he would mind picking them up and bringing them into the house.

When he picked the boxes up, I screamed, "A snake!!!"

He dropped the boxes and the snake landed on the porch and slithered away into the bushes.

"Thank you, Lord. You want those flags up and by Your grace they WILL fly and by Your grace we WILL continue to read Your word from our county courthouse."

Chapter 21 - DEFINITELY NOT MISTAKEN IDENTITY

"I will instruct thee and teach thee in the way which thou shalt go:
I will guide thee with mine eye."
Psalm 32:8

Figure 57 - LAURA WILLIAMS BRM COORDINATOR, NIGERIA

Sometime in 2009 I received a friend request from a lady by the name of Laura Williams. I thought this was quite unique since one of my dearest friends in Cochran is Laura Williams, a pastor's wife.

The reason I found this so unique was because the lady who friended me was not only African, she was from Nigeria, Africa. I accepted her friend request and as far as I can tell she never once commented on any of my posts in eight years, or for that matter hit "like" on anything I posted.

In January of 2018 I received a private message from her on FB asking me to send her material on how to start a Bible Reading Marathon. She had apparently been reading my posts about our local BRM; but I was a bit taken aback by her request since she was from Nigeria.

Who of us has not heard about money scams coming out of Nigeria? I immediately looked to see who our mutual friends were and to my surprise we only had one mutual friend, but it couldn't have been a better one.

Victor Strysky, our mutual friend, was greatly influenced to give his life to Christ, by the same person that brought my family to the Lord back in the '50s. Victor was not only a Christian, but he and I had been good friends for many years, and he is also one of the National Directors under Pastor John Hagee's ministry, Christians United For Israel (CUFI).

I asked Victor if she was okay (meaning she's not a scam artist) and without a second's hesitation he said, "She's fine! No problem." I breathed a sigh of relief and sent her all the information on starting the first Bible Reading Marathon in Lagos, Nigeria.

Laura, it turns out, is an incredible soldier for the Lord. She heads up a ministry to 500 widows and is a member of one of the largest, if not THE largest church in the world. (Redeemed Christian Church of God, Inc.)

She promptly sent me two pages of prayer requests, including prayers concerning the two terrorist groups in Nigeria: Boko Haram and Felani Herdsmen.

I was stunned when I received the prayer requests. This woman was serious about prayer. I had much to learn from her about walking by faith.

Definitely Not Mistaken Identity

At the time all this was happening I was in the middle of teaching 37 ladies Hebrew at our RSAT facility. Believe it or not, there were enough prayer requests to give each lady an individual prayer request on a special prayer card with Laura's picture. In this way they could *see* the woman they were praying for and pray they did!

Figure 58 - FEAR IS A LIAR ROCK

I had heard about the Boko Haram terrorist group kidnapping some young schoolgirls, but that had been quite a few years prior to this contact with Laura and I started toying with the idea of traveling to Nigeria . . . that is until another round of kidnappings took place.

We were only a month into praying for Laura and her many prayer requests when, on February 19th, a faction of Boko Haram went into the northeast Nigerian town of Dapchi and kidnapped 110 female students from a Science and Technical College.

Oops! Changed my mind on that trip.

On May 1st I received another private message from Laura, and it shook me to my core. She invited me to come to the opening of their very first Bible Reading Marathon in Lagos! We had not discussed this possibility. In fact, I hadn't even mentioned my thoughts to Charlie about going.

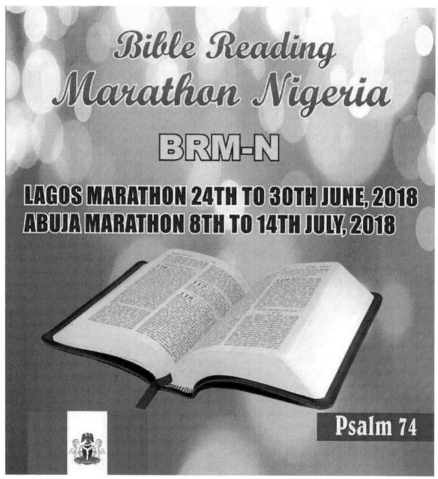

Figure 59 - POSTER FOR BRM NIGERIA

When Charlie read her message, I was shocked when he said, "Well, we'll pray about it and if we feel it's safe you can go." What?

I was stunned that he would even consider me going to Nigeria, but I also realized this might be God, since being open to something like this was a bit unlike him.

Definitely Not Mistaken Identity

On the night of May 2nd, we were plowing ahead on our last night of the 90-hour marathon. A good friend dropped by the courthouse and while the readings were continuing, she and I were quietly talking and visiting. I mentioned that I was going to try and get people reading the Bible in different languages the following year.

She responded enthusiastically and said, "That would be wonderful. I have a friend who just moved here from Nigeria and He could read the Bible in his language."

That was the last thing I expected from her and when she left the plaza I sat down on a bench in front of the courthouse, pondering this whole Nigerian thing. As soon as I sat down a young woman, Stacey Brady, who was also sitting on the bench, said, "Jerri, have you seen the little rocks I've been painting and putting all around the courthouse?"

I told her I had and that they were very cute. She then pointed to a bush and said, "Have you seen that one?" I got up and walked over to the bush and picked up the painted rock. The message on the rock said, *FEAR IS A LIAR.*

There is no way I can tell you how the message on that little rock spoke to me. In fact, I took it home and have it prominently displayed on a bookcase. From that very second ALL fear left my heart about going to Nigeria.

May 3rd and the marathon was over. Late that night I called my brother Doug Krieger, who lives in California, to tell him how wonderful the marathon had gone. I was exhausted and all thoughts of Nigeria were put on a back burner somewhere in my brain!

He answered with a loud whisper, "What do you want?"

"Excuse me? What did you say?" I asked, puzzled.

"What do you want, Jerri?" he whispered loudly again.

"Are you in a meeting or something?" I asked.

"Yes! I'm listening to some Nigerian brothers singing." He held up his cell phone so I could hear them too.

Figure 60 - PRESENTED BRM CERTIFICATE FOR READING THE BIBLE TO JOSHUA MEETING

To say I was stunned was an understatement. I told him goodbye and that I would call him the next day and flopped into bed, totally exhausted physically and mentally. "Whatever, Lord."

The next day I discovered that Doug's friend, Henry Hon, had just been to Nigeria on a mission trip and he had recorded some Nigerian brothers singing in a church service. When I told my brother that I had been invited to go to Nigeria he was quite excited and said he would pray with me about a possible trip.

The wheels were turning. Charlie and I started praying in earnest. Along with our prayers came some details that had to be worked out. My passport had expired, so that was one hurdle to jump. I also needed vaccinations required for travel to Africa. Following all of that, there would be a visa to procure, *PLUS* I was just winding up the 16-week Hebrew course at RSAT.

Definitely Not Mistaken Identity

A few days before we were to drive down to Savannah (3-hour trip), I needed to go into town and see a friend who ran a beauty shop. I parked the car across the street from her shop and as I went to step up onto the sidewalk, I had a horrible fall on my left hip. Instantly I thought, "Oh, no. My hip is broken!"

Ladies in the beauty shop saw the fall and came running outside. Let me tell you, it was quite the scene. I was telling them I was fine in the name of Jesus and to help me get up and they were saying, "No! No! You can't get up. We've called an ambulance and the police."

In that instant I knew that if I were to go to the hospital there would be no trip to Nigeria and no graduation that week for 37 beautiful ladies at RSAT. "Get me up," I yelled. "I'm fine in the name of Jesus!"

It started to rain and one of the women brought out an umbrella, while they continued to try to keep me calm. Calm wasn't happening. "Are you guys crazy," I said. "It's raining. Get me up!"

They gave in and got me into the beauty shop. I didn't see the police officer until I said, "I'm out of here."

The officer looked at me with a stern face and said, "No, you're not lady. You're not going anywhere until the ambulance gets here."

In a few minutes Heartland Ambulance Service drove up and I walked outside. To their astonishment I lifted my left leg high up in the air in front of me and then lifted it up behind me and said, "I'm fine! If my hip was broken, I couldn't do that, now could I?"

As they stood gaping at me, I walked back across the street and got in my little pickup truck and drove off. As I continued down the street, I heard the Lord whisper in my spirit, "That was a test and you passed it."

Figure 61 - THEY TRAVELED THREE HOURS TO READ THE BIBLE

The following day, I was still hurting, but we made it to Savannah where I got my yellow fever vaccination. The next day when I woke up my wrist and forearm were terribly swollen. The pain was intense. I pointed at my wrist and arm and said, "In the name of Jesus . . . swelling go down!" And it did.

The next day was Thursday and we had a fantastic graduation at RSAT. The 37 ladies paraded down the center aisle in graduation caps and gowns to Israeli music played on a CD player. They sang, read and spoke in Hebrew as their prayer partners rejoiced with them in their great accomplishment. I was so proud of them.

My pain was virtually gone the next day and the following month I was off to Nigeria! I'm so glad I accepted that friend request from Laura Williams in Nigeria. My acceptance of her request to be my Facebook friend was *NOT* a case of mistaken identity, but a case of *GOD* identity!

Chapter 22 - HOW DO YOU EAT AN ELEPHANT?

"If my people, which are called by my name, shall humble themselves, and pray, and seek my face, and turn from their wicked ways; then will I hear from heaven, and will forgive their sin, and will heal their land."
2 Chronicles 7:14

> "If My people who are called by My name will humble themselves, and pray and seek My face, and turn from their wicked ways, then I will hear from heaven, and will forgive their sin and heal their land."
> 2 Chronicles 7:14
>
> BRM 7/14 PROJECT

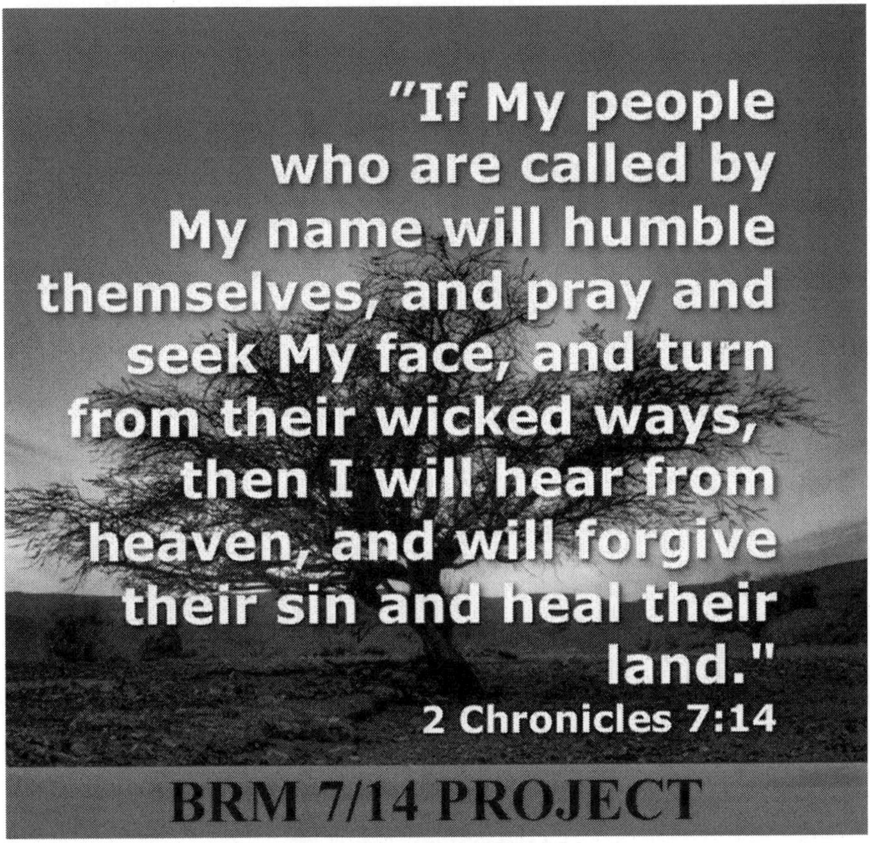

Figure 62 - 2 CHRONICLES 7:14

What an amazing time I had participating in Lagos, Nigeria's first Bible Reading Marathon. My hostess, Laura Williams, was incredible! She had participants scheduled to read from at least four different states in Nigeria.

The interest was so great that she has had at least four more Bible Reading Marathons in the past year. Participants from all over Nigeria are reading and then reporting on their

What's App program what they've read, along with a picture of them reading.

I'm on the BRMN (Bible Reading Marathon Nigeria) call and so my phone gives a little 'ding' each time a portion is read. What a blessing to see the word of God being read all over Nigeria.

In March of 2019 I received a private message on FB from Laura asking me if I knew of anyone in Des Moines, Iowa that could host friends of hers for approximately two weeks. Her friends had a son graduating from the university and they needed a place to stay. The man was a Nigerian pastor and worthy of all the help Laura could get for him and his wife.

I told her that, not only did I not know anyone in Des Moines, Iowa . . . I didn't know anyone in the entire state of Iowa, but that I would pray. There's that word again . . . *PRAY*!

Surprise might be an understatement to what I felt when a lady contacted me from Des Moines, Iowa that night! Dianne Bentley had put the words "Bible Reading Marathon" into a Google search and came up with my name. Wow!

Backtracking just a little to explain why my name was on a Google search: it was due to all the flack I got for flying the Christian flag in our town and having a Bible Reading Marathon at our courthouse. Although the atheists sought to disgrace and stop my efforts in spreading the Word of God, they instead did me a huge favor! Their efforts to stop God's word turned out to be the cause to spread it even further!

(I think I read somewhere that *all things work together for good, for those who love God and are called according to His purpose.*)

But . . . I digress.

Dianne, it turns out, is the Iowa State leader for Bible Reading Marathons. In 2018 she divided the Bible into 99 equal reading portions to correlate with Iowa's 99 counties. Then on

July 14 (7/14) at 7:14 a.m. all the county readers assembled at their courthouses and read their assigned portions . . . thus having the entire Bible read at the same time statewide.

Figure 63 - DIANNE BENTLEY FROM IOWA

All this was done in connection with 2 Chronicles 7:14. Dianne was on a search to get other states to join her in this project.

My spirit literally leaped with excitement. There was no way this contact was a coincidence. This was a God moment and I was on board immediately!

While discussing all of this with Dianne I mentioned the couple from Nigeria who needed a place to stay for several weeks. Dianne assured me she would pray about this and let me know. I contacted Laura and we prayed that if God wanted Dianne to help that He would lay it on her heart.

Not wanting to waste a minute of time I divided the Bible into 159 even portions and started the process of getting volunteers to read from Georgia's 159 counties. I already had contacts in five other counties who had begun Bible Reading Marathons, but that still left over 150 to contact! Wouldn't you know ... Georgia is 2nd only to Texas in the number of counties.

Now I was not only praying for housing for the Nigerian couple, I was also praying about how to contact someone in every county in Georgia. Looking at a county map, the task seemed enormous, but I knew it was possible because I knew the contact from Des Moines, Iowa was from God. And by the way, did I mention I was in the middle of organizing Cochran's 16th Annual Bible Reading Marathon?

Figure 64 - GOD'S WORD OVER THE WORLD - JULY 14

A Bible Reading Marathon has 90 hours of reading. From the very first Bible Reading Marathon in 2004, when a young woman volunteered to read for five hours, I've never stressed out about getting readers.

This year (2019) I had the entire 90 hours of reading filled up one month in advance! This was unheard of and I was thrilled. The next day, after getting the final commitment for readers for our 16th BRM, I said a little prayer that went something like this: "Lord, what do you want me to do today?" As I was getting ready for church, I clicked the Bible App on my phone and the daily Scripture was 2 Chronicles 7:14. I had my answer. The 7/14 Bible Reading Project was to be my priority.

Several weeks went by and I was up to 20 counties who had signed up for the BRM 7/14 project. Then Dianne called from Iowa to share that she and her husband and several others had been praying for the couple in Nigeria and they felt God wanted them to help them. Praise God! I sent the information off to Laura and got back to work on the 7/14 project.

A month had gone by and I had nearly half the counties in Georgia signed up. Up to this juncture all work on the project was done through prayer, word of mouth and Facebook posts. I began receiving calls from all over Georgia. One man asked me, "How do you know someone in every county in Georgia."

I laughed and said, "What are you talking about? I don't even know who YOU are!"

I began filling in a statewide county map of Georgia with yellow markers. My husband would give a laugh when I would yell from my computer room, "Got another one!" This went on day after day.

When I would begin to get bogged down with how big the task looked, Charlie would remind me, "Remember how you eat an elephant! One bite at a time."

Midway through my efforts I had an opportunity to share about the 7/14 project on an Atlanta Live TV program. I held up my little county map and asked the TV audience to pray. Later, when the project was completely over, I discovered how powerful were the prayers of that TV audience.

My brother, Doug Krieger, was in a restaurant in Sacramento, California. He struck up a conversation with a couple of men seated nearby. When he found out that one of the men was from Atlanta, Georgia he told them his sister had just had an exciting statewide Bible Reading Marathon there.

Figure 65 - JERRI WITH COUNTY MAP OF GEORGIA

One of the men said, "I know who your sister is."

My brother was dumbfounded. "You know who my sister is?"

"Yes," he replied. "Your sister is Jerri Tuck. We saw her on TV with a map of Georgia and we heard her share about the 7/14 project. We prayed she would get all the counties signed up. When we saw her the second time on the same program, we rejoiced that she had every county signed up to read."

How Do You Eat An Elephant?

The day finally arrived. The entire Bible was read over the state of Georgia in an hour or less. Reports began to pour in of the blessings people experienced by reading the Bible, knowing others in every county in Georgia were also involved.

In one instance a man drove three hours to read in a county in which no reader had been assigned. Steve MacGregor, a true servant of God, was not going to let that happen. When he discovered there was no one reading in this county he got up extra early and was at the courthouse at 7 a.m., joining the statewide readings.

An inmate in a women's prison found out about the project and found out the assigned reading for her county and, behind the razor wire, read the portion of Scripture. She wrote to friends about the experience. Her letter in part reads:

I participated in the BRM today here at Pulaski State Prison and I was so blessed by just being able to be a part of this. I thank you so much and I thank God for you as well. This week has been not been one of my best and with the BRM and my personal study of Ezekiel 43 yesterday the Lord has greatly lifted my spirit and reminded me who I am in Him and to Him and who I will be for Him. I thank you and appreciate this so much, you have no idea. This event will bless or rather has blessed so many people today. I don't know when you will be doing this again, but count me in. Thank you again and may God bless you.

As a result of this letter the Statewide Bible Reading next year, in 2020, will also include every Georgia State Prison! County leaders, Steve MacGregor, Jimmy Welchel, and Jeremy Stroop, Chaplain at Walker State Prison, will be heading up the newest project: 7/14 Bible Reading Marathon Behind the Razor Wire!

Thanks be to God! We ate the whole elephant!

Everything by Prayer

Chapter 23 - THREE RESURRECTIONS

"And you He made alive, who were dead in trespasses and sins,"
Ephesians 2:1

Figure 66 - BLECKLEY PROBATION DETENTION CENTER - COCHRAN

As I come to an end of sharing great answers to prayer, I was reminded of something from the New Testament. We read of only three accounts of the Lord Jesus raising people from the dead.

First, there was a 12-year old girl (Mark 5:35-43); then a young man (Luke 7:11-16); then an older man (John 11: 21-44).

All were dead, unable to move, speak, hear or respond in any way. However, all were different ages and at different stages of death. The little girl had just died and was still at home in her bed; the young man was being carried to his final resting place in a funeral procession and the older man had already been buried and had been in the grave for four days.

Resurrection life returned to all three by the power of the words coming out of the mouth of the Lord Jesus Christ. All were notable miracles, but you can be assured these were not the only persons that Jesus raised from the dead, but these three were written for a specific reason.

John, the beloved Apostle, wrote, *"And many other signs truly did Jesus in the presence of his disciples, which are not written in this book: But these are written, that ye might believe that Jesus is the Christ, the Son of God; and that believing ye might have life through his name"* (John 20:31-32).

I believe that one of the reasons might be that they were examples of various stages of life when they each died, and yet . . . dead is still dead! Jesus has the power, no matter how long one has been dead in sin, to raise them up into new life!

Allow me to share about three resurrections I witnessed in the prison system. Charlie and I have been so blessed to be prison volunteers. We have seen much in our 30+ years of prison ministry, but the following three accounts were quite astounding.

When the Bleckley Probation Detention Center first opened 16 years ago in Cochran there were women detainees who were incarcerated. Then followed a changeover and the women were transferred out of the facility and men were now housed at the Bleckley PDC.

Men or women didn't make any difference to us. We knew everyone needs Jesus and we just counted it a privilege to be able to share the Good News with the men as we had with the women.

One night there were about 60 men in attendance and at the conclusion of the Bible study I had the men stand for prayer. "Before I close in prayer," I said, "I'm going to read your names off the sign-in roster."

This was something I had never done before, but I felt the impression of the Holy Spirit to read all the names and leave one off at random. After reading the names I asked, "Did everyone hear their name?"

The men began shaking their heads affirmatively and looking at the man next to them and saying, "I heard mine. Did you hear yours?"

"Who is Mr. Coby Daniel?" I asked.

A man on the very back row raised his hand.

"Mr. Daniel did you know that one day the roll will be called up yonder and if your name is not on that roll you won't be going into Heaven? Are you saved, Mr. Daniel?" He shook his head indicating he was not saved.

"Mr. Daniel, would you like to be saved?" He answered that he would and so I asked him to come to the front.

While two inmates laid their hands on his shoulders and joined me in prayer, Coby Daniel gave his heart to Christ. What a thunderous applause from all the men.

The next night at 2 a.m. the lights were turned on in all four dorms and the announcement was made: "Attention everyone! Get all your things together. You're moving out!"

What a shock! No one had any idea this was going to happen, but God certainly did, and He was giving Coby Daniel a chance at new life in Christ.

Three or four months went by and I was 'friended' on Facebook by a stranger. I usually just delete these requests by persons I don't know, but for some reason I couldn't do so and when I finally accepted the request it was Coby Daniel. By now I had totally forgotten his name, but again . . . God hadn't forgotten Coby.

What a joy to find out that he was no longer an inmate, but was a free man, serving the Lord. He and his wife and baby lived several hours from Cochran. Charlie and I drove up to see him at his home in Thomaston and had a blessed time of fellowship. This happened years ago. Since that time Coby has become a licensed minister of the gospel and was one of our county leaders for our 7/14 Bible Reading Marathon project.

Women are now incarcerated at the facility that has been changed from a detention center to a rehabilitation center known as RSAT. The women are sentenced to nine months at the Residential Substance Abuse Treatment center and they attend school four days a week during this period.

We had taught one Hebrew course to the men and now the opportunity was presented to the women. The course is a simple course designed to familiarize the students with the Hebrew alphabet. The course is 16 weeks and for those who are still serving time we offer an advanced course which leads them into a deeper meaning of the Hebrew alphabet. This attendance is usually much smaller because so many of the women in the first course are graduating out of RSAT.

Figure 67 - COBY AND DOROTHY DANIEL

Three Resurrections

One Friday afternoon during the advanced class, which had only six women enrolled, Mr. Tommy Bowen the RSAT Superintendent dropped in. He usually would come in for a few minutes just to let the ladies know he was so proud of them for taking the advanced course.

On this Friday the ladies were sitting in a semi-circle in front of me when, without any warning, there was a supersonic boom!!! It was so loud the windows rattled.

Laughing I raised my hand and said, "Ladies, that's how fast the Lord is going to come. I'm sure glad we're all saved, except maybe Mr. Bowen," I laughed.

Mr. Bowen protested and said, "I'm going too!"

I looked around at the women and saw that only one woman didn't have her hand raised up. "Tabatha," I asked, "Aren't you saved?"

She shook her head and with a downcast look answered, "No, ma'am."

I didn't want to make an issue of it and just smiled and finished teaching the lesson, but you can rest assured I really prayed for Tabatha that night.

The following morning as I was again praying for her I was reading my Bible and in my regular reading schedule I came to Acts 9:36-41. I was stunned. The spelling differed by one letter, but the account is of a dead woman by the name of Tabitha whom Peter raised from the dead. I was ecstatic. God was going to save Tabatha!

The following week I was holding a Bible study at RSAT with about 30 women in attendance. Tabatha came up to me when the class was over and said, "Well, I'm ready!"

I feigned ignorance. "Ready for what?"

"I'm ready to get saved!"

Believe me there was rejoicing in the presence of the angels of God that night and in the Tuck household when I shared with Charlie what had happened.

I'm sure you remember Martha's words to Jesus when she heard him say to roll the stone away from the tomb in which her brother had lain for four days, *"Lord by this time there is a terrible stench."* In good old King James English (KJV) it says, *"By this time he stinketh."*

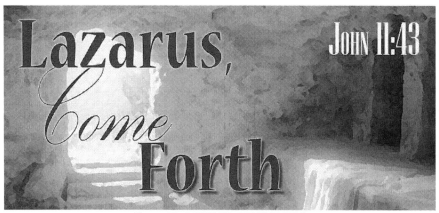

Figure 68 - LAZARUS, COME FORTH!

Some have been sinners for many, many days but that means nothing to Jesus. He died for everyone, regardless of how bad they've become.

In one of our regular meetings at Dooly Prison, a men's facility in Unadilla, Georgia we had a very interesting meeting.

As the men came into the meeting room, it was Charlie's habit to shake hands and welcome each man to the meeting. My job was to preach. We had a very good-sized crowd with 178 men in attendance.

There was no way I couldn't notice a man on the back row whose face and head were completely covered with tattoos. As I preached the word I was also praying for the man and thinking, "Wow! When he gets saved, he's going to need a telephone job."

Of course, there was no way I could point the man out, but just as I was ending my message he stood up, grabbed his waistband and seemingly straightened his pants and then sat back down.

This was my chance!

"Young man on the back row," I said. "Did you have a question?"

"NO!" he said gruffly.

"Then I have a question for you," I said. "Are you saved?"

"NO!"

"Would you like to be saved?" (I guess I was thinking about Coby Daniel)

"NO!"

"Fine. Thank you very much." Then I just went back to finishing up the message and dismissed the men.

When we got out to the truck my husband said, "Honey when that guy came in, he didn't want to shake my hand, but I grabbed it anyway and welcomed him to the meeting. He looked me dead in the eye and said, 'I just want you to know the devil is with you tonight in this meeting.'"

Whoa! Talk about prayers. I immediately sent private prayer requests out to dozens of my prayer partners. I called him the, *Tattoo Man*.

A few weeks later we were at the prison for a graduation when an inmate came up to me and asked me if I remembered the *Tattoo Man*. I told him I certainly did.

He then informed me that the inmate had gotten saved! What?

"Yes, ma'am. He came up to me about a week after that meeting and said he decided to get saved, but that he was going to wait until Mrs. Tuck came back to get saved when she was here."

The inmate told the *Tattoo Man* he didn't need to put it off because we never know what a day will bring forth. (Proverbs 27:1) The inmate prayed with the *Tattoo Man* and he was saved!

Three sinners . . . three resurrections . . . and yet I know there will be many, many more. Our job is to preach the Word of God and PRAY!

Chapter 24 - MAKING LIFE COUNT FOR ETERNITY

*"For what shall it profit a man,
if he shall gain the whole world,
and lose his own soul?"*
Mark 8:36

I hope you've enjoyed this trip down the Tuck memory lane. As I approach the completion of my 80th year on this planet I am so grateful that God has shown His mercy toward me in so many ways.

No one realizes more than I what a merciful and gracious God we serve. At age 15 I ran away and got married. Shortly after I got married my husband was called to serve his country overseas. While he was in Okinawa, I started riding motorcycles with the Hell's Angels. This led to one sin after another until I got caught up in a bizarre life by living with a gangster! My life was spiraling out of control.

Enter the grace of God! My stepmother and my father got saved and they started praying for me. Along with their prayers, were the prayers of the people in a weekly Bible study they attended, plus the prayers of a grandmother who lived in South Dakota.

Prayer works!

At age 17 I went to the home Bible study as a totally lost sinner on her way to hell. When I left that evening, I was a new creation in Christ and my life was never to be the same.

My thirst for the things of God has not diminished in the least. As I write this book, I have been walking with God for nearly 63 years. In all these years I have been blessed beyond my wildest dreams.

There were sad times; the death of my firstborn child, a marriage that ended in divorce after nearly 17 years, disappointments and misunderstandings and a host of other things that I

Everything by Prayer

had to take to the Lord in prayer. In every instance, God granted me grace and strength to face another day.

For the past 47 years I have been blessed to be married to the most wonderful man in the world. His salvation was also an answer to a mother's prayers. When I met his mom over the telephone I commented, "I bet you prayed a lot for Charlie."

With a West Virginia twang she said, "I carried that boy 'round my neck for 18 years!" I got a good laugh out of that one, but I also was reminded that both Charlie and I were blessed to have faithful prayer warriors who prayed us into the kingdom.

As we come to the end of our brief journey here on earth, we are mindful of the brevity of life. Famous missionary to the Auca Indians in Ecuador, Jim Elliot said, "He is no fool who gives what he cannot keep, to gain what he cannot lose."

We can't take anything with us into eternity except souls. We have been blessed with a lot materially, but we are very aware that we will leave it all behind. C.T. Studd, missionary to Africa and India, said, "Only one life, t'will soon be past. Only what's done for Christ will last." How true.

Considering what these two missionaries, who are now with the Lord, have said, may we do everything we can to make our lives count for eternity.

Do not be over-anxious about anything, but by prayer and earnest pleading, together with thanksgiving, let your request be unreservedly made known in the presence of God.

Philippians 4:6 (Weymouth NT)

"Then another angel, having a golden censer, came and stood at the altar. He was given much incense, that he should offer it with the prayers of all the saints upon the golden altar which was before the throne. And the smoke of the incense, with the prayers of the saints, ascended before God from the angel's hand."

Revelation 8:3-4 (NKJV)

About the Author & Jerri's Books

Jerri Tuck has served her Lord with passion and fervor since accepting Christ in February of 1957. In her B.C. days she rode with the notorious Hell's Angels motorcycle gang in California. A dramatic encounter with Jesus in a home Bible study changed the direction of her life.

Immediately after her conversion experience in 1957, Jerri began to serve the Lord, working as a teacher with Child Evangelism Fellowship and eventually became a trainer of teachers. Hundreds of boys and girls came to salvation through her outreach in weekly Good News Clubs from California to Pennsylvania.

Yes, Jerri's been fishing for souls taking her into prisons and foreign lands and to her second church, Walmart, where she inevitably catches souls for Jesus coming and going and while shopping around in the store. This is a great reason to write *Gone Fishin'* which tells in 31 devotional encounters how these fish were caught for her Lord and Savior.

Many twists and turns along in her journey with her Lord,

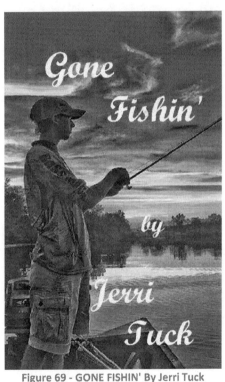

Figure 69 - GONE FISHIN' By Jerri Tuck

brought Jerri through some deep waters. When her first marriage finally ended, she found herself in hopeless straights; but the Lord ended that which was "unequally yoked" prior to her salvation and gave her a new husband, Charlie, whose love for Christ matched Jerri's. Together their 47-year marriage has raised 9 children in their old farmhouse in Central Georgia—that's why her book, **Patchwork Family**, is a must read!

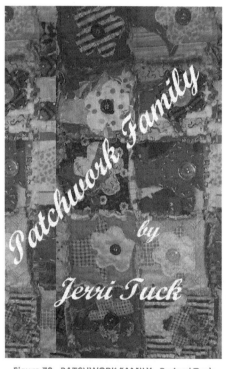

Figure 70 - PATCHWORK FAMILY - By Jerri Tuck

Shortly after moving from California to Georgia in 1974 she became involved with the Women's Aglow Fellowship International. From holding monthly Aglow meetings in her hometown of Cochran she became the president of the Central Georgia Women's Aglow Area Board.

In her secular career she has been a disc jockey with radio station WVMG, a feature writer and reporter for the Macon Telegraph & News, and a successful real estate broker and appraiser for 28 years.

Her foreign mission work has included missionary trips to Brazil, India, Ecuador, Mexico, China, Costa Rica and working for a Jewish organization (Ser-El), volunteering to help the Israeli Defense Force (IDF) in Israel.

Author's Page

Since 1997 she has written a weekly column entitled *Just Jerri*. A portion of her hundreds of articles was compiled and turned into another book entitled, you guessed it: *JUST JERRI* . . . a terrific devotional of everyday life experiences where Jesus just shows up and extends His love and peace in the midst of some of the most turbulent circumstances.

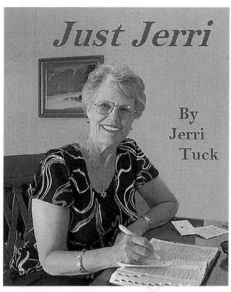

Figure 71 - "JUST JERRI" - By Jerri Tuck

Earlier in 2004 Jerri started the first Bible Reading Marathon in the state of Georgia through the International Bible Reading Association. This has continued every year since and has been spreading to other counties in Georgia

Jerri is currently serving on the board of the Bleckley Christian Learning Center (BCLC) and is also a substitute teacher for the organization. BCLC is in its fourth year of holding Bible classes in the Bleckley County public school system. She is also secretary for the Cochran-Bleckley Ministerial Alliance and is the Coordinator for all the Christian meetings held at the Residential Substance Abuse Treatment Center (RSAT) in Cochran.

On August 6, 2004 Jerri was honored at a special ceremony in San Antonio, Texas as one of only 17 women throughout the world in the Church of God in that year, to be inducted into the Hall of Christian Excellence through the COG Women's Ministries.

Figure 72 - LETTER FOR THE COG HALL OF CHRISTIAN EXCELLENCE 2004

When God said, *"Who will go for Us?"* her response was immediate... *"Here am I, Lord. Send me."*

(Jerri and her husband Charlie have been married 47 years. They have 9 children, 22 grandchildren and 15 great-grandchildren. They make their home in Cochran, GA. Charlie was the Chief Appraiser for Bleckley County and is also retired.)

Author's Page

Figure 73 - CHARLIE & JERRI TUCK - NEARLY 50 YEARS SERVING THE LORD

To contact Jerri go to her Facebook page: www.facebook.com/jerri.tuck.75, or email her at: jerrituck@aol.com if you are interested in her books.

*Be anxious for nothing, but in **everything by prayer** and supplication with thanksgiving let your requests be made known to God.*
Philippians 4:6

Made in the USA
Columbia, SC
09 August 2023